Walking In My Destiny

Driven by Faith

WOMEN'S COMPILATION PROJECT

Volume 4

Featuring:

LaSandré C. Bush
Linda Bush
Arna Erega
Takilla Florence
Kimberly Mihalik
L'Tarra Moore
Jennifer Rodriguez
Loretta Scott
Tracey L. Sigers
LaTrice D. Snodgrass
LaVonia M. Thompson
Carolyn Treadwell
Missy Watts-Rodriguez

Published by
Again I Rise Publishing
Chicago, Illinois

Printed in the United States of America

ISBN: 9780998614830

Library of Congress Control Number: 2018933304

Cover and Interior Design by Jessica Tilles/TWA Solutions

All stories appear courtesy of the authors, unless otherwise noted.

Scriptures used are taken from the New King James Version Bible.

The Women's Compilation Project is hosted by Mutual Partners Association, which is nonprofit organization that implement after-school and summer programs for youth in urban communities. The proceeds from this book will help pay for youth to attend after-school and summer programs that teach character development, self-esteem, leadership skills and experiential learning through fun activities such as theater, music, art, dance and sports.

Acknowledgments

First and foremost, I would like to thank my Lord and Savior Jesus Christ for entrusting me with this project. Truly, without Him none of this would have been possible.

I would like to thank my mother, Mary Loretta Burns, for her love and support. You are an amazing woman who has taught me to be giving, loving, and compassionate toward others. Mom you have been my lifetime support system and I appreciate the love you show me daily. I love you with all my heart.

I am very grateful for my husband, Abdoulaye Diarrassouba, who supports me, loves me, and encourages me daily. God truly blessed me the day we met.

I would like to thank my late father, Leroy Tripplett, who always believed in me. Whenever I thought I could not do something, he would say, "Baby, you can do it." He was such a wonderful dad who taught me the philosophy of life and how to live life intentionally.

I would like to thank my brother, Ricardo Burns, for always being by my side through thick and thin. You are my rock!

I would like to thank all the women who participated in The Women's Compilation Project. I do not take your participation lightly. You opened your hearts to this project and have trusted me throughout the process of creating this book.

I would be remiss not to mention my editor, Jessica Tilles, who has worked on every compilation book project. She is awesome and good at what she does. Thank you, Jessica.

Bridget Burns-Diarrassouba
Publisher

Acknowledgments from some of the authors...

I would like to express my gratitude to Bridget Diarrassouba for the opportunity to collaborate with such a phenomenal group of women. I would also like to thank all those who assisted in the editing, proofreading, design, and publication of this project. Last, but not least, I would like to thank my daddy for his continual affirmation of the endless possibilities for my life. His love gave me the strength to find comfort in my discomfort and passion to help others as I help myself deal with the loudness of the silence.

— *LaTrice Snodgrass*

I cannot express enough thanks to God, the creator of my life. To my pastor, Elder Willie Priester, and his wife, Evangelist Dell Priester, for sound doctrine teaching of God's Word. To Apostle Robert E. Crosby for the words of encouragement and the push to move forward. To everyone that believed in me and, most importantly, I am grateful to all of those whom I had the pleasure to work with during this project.

— *Linda Bush*

I want to acknowledge my mom for making all the difficult decisions as she was raising me and my brother and for never making a mistake! Thank you for instilling the values I hold today and for showing me that I, too, can be a super woman! Thank you to my brother, Andi, who continues to teach me how to love and give unconditionally! And, thank you to my dad, who relieved me by saying that the world will not come to an end if I don't break the magic barrier of 13 seconds in 100 meter hurdles!

— *Arna Erega*

A special thank you to my children, Lakisha, Joey, and Garland, for giving me the faith and drive to wake up every morning. I also wish to express special gratitude to Bridgett for her tenacity to put forth this work and her commitment to help others; and to the editor, Jessica Tilles for, her editorial suggestions and depth of knowledge, and for putting my words into action. Most of all, I want to thank all the mothers, whose silent cry that never goes unnoticed. I hear you.

— Loretta Scott

I would like to acknowledge every woman in my life, past and present, who has ever planted a positive seed in my journey. Those seeds have manifested into the woman that you are supporting today. I would also like to dedicate this book to anyone that has ever thought about giving up on life. This book is proof that God can do all things except fail! I pray that as you read this book, you will find strength and comfort in the words.

— Takilla Florence

My story in this compilation is dedicated to my mother, Sharon Y. Williams, because of her love and strength. She has always been the person I bounce ideas off and she always gives me the brutal, honest, truth, even when I didn't want to hear it. She is the strongest woman I know and an excellent role model. Thank you, Mom, for being my truth and believing in me always! I love you, Mom!

— LaSandré Bush

Table of Contents

LaSandré C. Bush
Ready. Set. Momentum! 1

Linda C. Bush
Faith Through Tragedy 9

Arna Erega
Through Perseverance to Freedom 19

Takilla Florence
Formed in the Womb 29

Kimberly S. Mihalik
Running Toward His Grace 37

L'Tarra Moore
There is Moore 47

Jennifer Rodriguez
Piece by Piece 55

Loretta Scott
A Mother's Cry 65

Tracey L. Siegers
Confessions of a Beauty Queen: "Design Essentials" 73

LaTrice D. Snodgrass
When the Silence is Too Loud 83

LaVonia M. Thompson
No Matter What, He Still Loves You 91

Caroyln Treadwell
Get Out! Live Your Life Intentionally 101

Missy Watts-Rodriguez
Broken No More 111

Write Your Own Story 119

LASANDRÉ C. BUSH

Ready. Set. Momentum!

LASANDRÉ C. BUSH

Ready. Set. Momentum!

Life appeared to be perfect. My career was flourishing rapidly, I was married to my college sweetheart, with one beautiful daughter and another on the way. I had the luxury vehicles, a nice four-bedroom, two-car garage starter home and a loving, supportive family. In the midst of giving birth to my second daughter, I blacked out. When I awoke, my physician greeted me with the words, "You will no longer be able to have children."

Confusion, disbelief, and anger were the cause of tears streaming heavily down my face. The physician must have mistaken me for someone else. As the anesthesia was wearing off, I remembered being in labor and I hadn't seen my baby yet. I distinctly remembered before labor, I was praying and having a conversation with my husband.

"If anything happens to me, my father, or the baby, please do not keep it from me," I told him.

While in labor, my father was dealing with an illness that was slowly claiming his life. Every time my phone rang, I would get tense because I never knew what might come next because of his health. I was the oldest, strongest, and the one who had to keep it together for my younger sisters and mother. In the meantime, the intense labor pains continued and as soon as my physician's shift started, I was up for an impromptu cesarean.

While being wheeled down the hallway, I reminded my husband, "Don't look when they cut me open. I need you not to pass out."

It was time to deliver; the spinal anesthesia injected, sheet raised, and the physician said, "All right, let's deliver baby number two for Mrs. Bush." This was familiar to him because he had delivered my first baby a year and a half prior, so I never stopped seeing him in the office for three straight years.

The pain was excruciating. I felt every cut, pull, and movement just beyond the sheet blocking my face. My tears and screaming were so intense; my husband hollering at the physician, "You better do something; my wife is in pain!" Then, I blacked out. I was under sedation for the remainder of the delivery. From what I understand, my husband exchanged a few more choice words. I saw my baby the next day after she was born.

Oh, but it got deeper. When I was informed I would not be able to have any more children, I instantly became angry because of the way it was delivered to me.

The physician said, "So, did your husband let you know what I said, not so much good news."

I answered, "Um, no."

He explained that I had a legitimate reason for hurting every single day, with excruciating pain after the first trimester. He told me that I had a uterine rupture, which only occurs in about one percent of women and is undetected via ultrasound. He said that if I would have carried any longer, the baby could have slipped into my abdomen, creating a severe bleed, which could have suffocated the baby. At that point, I was angry. Why was it that my husband knew all of this and hadn't spoken a word to me about this, when I had given specific instructions that if anything happened to tell me and not keep it from me? I questioned the physician several times about speaking with my husband about it. Of course, he took up for him and stated, "He probably didn't tell you because you would have several questions he couldn't answer." Now furious, I called my husband, whom was at home with the one-year-old, and went off.

Because his spirit is so kind, he just said, "Can we talk about it when I come back to the hospital? Just get some rest."

I couldn't believe I was forbidden to have any more children. I was in disbelief that my perfect life now had limitations. I never thought I would even have any, nor did I want any more after the difficulty I endured with my second pregnancy, but I wanted to make the decision, not be forced by the physician to take every precautionary measure not to get pregnant. That really put me in a state of ah, because he doesn't get to call the shots for my family and me.

My husband respects the idea of not having any more children because he knows it could be fatal for me and another child. On a couple occasions, he has mentioned how he would love to have a little boy and it makes me feel helpless, but he always says, "God is going to heal you and if you decide on trying for a boy, God will allow it and keep you and the baby." I realize every man wants a boy to carry on his legacy. I can also say that never in my life have I been on birth control, still practicing making babies often with my husband. If it happens, it is meant to be, and I will stay prayed up.

After my baby came home from the hospital, I went to stay with my parents to help out with my father who was battling a terminal illness. Along with a one-year-old and a newborn, my father and I were together for a strong three months. During that time, it wasn't about my healing from the cesarean. It was about taking care of them. I believe when I went back to work, I became complacent, and things started spinning out of control. My spending habit increased; I spent every lunch break at a different store, which regularly turned into a two-hour break because after shopping, I would sit down at any fine diner and have a nice large meal. Ultimately, my weight gain was out of control, I became sloppy and didn't care about how I dressed, never did my hair. I was fine with some gel and a high-school-girl ponytail. All of these things were out of character for me, but mommy mode had consumed my life. There wasn't time for anything else, not even a husband. I literally felt like I was having an out-of-body experience, disconnected from my own self with borderline depression, and didn't even know it. My perfect life was stripped away from me so much so that I didn't even recognize the perfect home or place of peace as it was supposed to be, it consumed my marriage and affect several other areas of my life as well.

An old friend schooled me on Psalms 68:19, *"Blessed the Lord, who daily loads us with benefits, even the God our salvation, Selah."*

Every day we have a new opportunity to plan and execute. I haven't been still the past three years, but I have been stagnant and comfortable. I found myself with no goals and just living day to day. It wasn't until I started approaching the thirty-year-old mark that I realized it and began wondering what happened. What do I have planned for the next ten years? What type of legacy will I leave for my children? What are my goals? Life is not perfect and that's okay. What isn't okay is giving up on yourself and giving up on your dreams. I thought I would be an accountant, but started working in healthcare and loved it. I made a career out of it and never looked back, but since time is of the essence, I shifted into gear and started thinking and making plans and goals.

Sometimes you have to find your *it* to push you and make you do things you only dreamed of. I walked into thirty with a surprise birthday party presented to me by my family with several of my closest friends and family. I walked out knowing I was cared about and loved. Still, I thought about my next move. I partnered with a business consultant and opened my own business: Sky Limits Credit Consultants, LLC in September 2017. I started a blog for my campaign: Spill Your Hot Sauce in December 2017, to promote woman entrepreneurship and goal execution. I'm sitting here now in December 2017 writing this book, which is 1 of 2 books I'm currently working on and I'm not stopping here. I have put together a strategic plan to scale and grow my business, my brand and stretch my momentum beyond my wildest dreams. I won't stop, I can't stop. As I quote in my campaign "It's time to spice things up." The fire has been lit and I'm burning my light brighter than ever. Keep God first, plan and execute the plan with intentional efforts daily. You can do whatever it is you want to do. Look, here it is, I don't believe in goals without deadlines. Your vision and purpose need to be aligned and your efforts *must* be intentional, with set milestones, in order for you to reach your ultimate goal. Yes, trials and tribulations will come, and you can quit every day, but when God reloads your benefits the next day, you *better* start again. As long as God gives you breath in your body, be intentional, be nice, and build relationships with the understanding that every encounter with everybody has the potential to possibly help you with your goals. Pray, be inspired, and keep the momentum!

Hello! I'm LaSandre' C. Bush, wife, mother and BOSS! I am an entrepreneur seeing explosive growth in my business and it has reignited a passion that I had to help others in their pursuit of personal excellence and professional success. I am also aspiring to become a Life Coach to accommodate my motivational speaking engagements and Authorship. There is a funny little story from years ago that caused my *Spill Your Hot Sauce* campaign. Though it sounds a little crazy when you hear, *Spill Your Hot Sauce*, it has a lot of meaning. Your Hot Sauce represents that thing inside you, that thing that if you just release it, it could change your life. It's time to spice things up ladies!

Visit me:
For any credit repair needs contact me at
www.Skylimitscredit.com

For daily motivation follow my *Spill Your Hot Sauce* blog at
www.spillyourhotsauce.wordpress.com

LINDA C. BUSH

Faith Through Tragedy

LINDA C. BUSH

Faith Through Tragedy

This thing called life has an unexpected way of bringing tragedies to all of us, and when you're least expecting it, things can happen and turn your world upside down. June 30, 2009 was one of the worst days of my life; it was a morning that I will never forget. I got up to get dressed for work, and afterward, stopped by my mother's room for a quick chat and then out the door. This was something that was routine for us, talking in the morning and calling one another at 12:00 p.m. (lunchtime) every day. I had been at work two and one-half hours when I received a call from my brother, screaming, "She's gone!"

I tried to figure out what he was talking about, so I asked, "What do you mean? Who's gone?"

He replied, "Mama's gone, Linda!"

In my mind, I thought, *Can't be; I just talked to her.*

I was working beside people on a production line at Allied Air Enterprise, making compressor parts for air conditioner units, and at the same time, trying to keep my sanity, even though my thoughts were crowding, my heart was pounding like it was about to come out of my chest, and my hands were trembling like I had the shakes. I left work, bubbling on the inside, tears streaming down my face, calling on the name of Jesus. "God! This can't be happening! No, Lord! No, Lord! Can't be! Where do I go from here? What do I do? Lord, You said You will never leave me nor forsake me; I need You now!"

Once I arrived at the hospital, and seeing my mother lying on the table, I just laid my head on her chest and cried. It was so unreal until the coroner came to pick up her body and reality kicked in.

After Mama's passing, when I thought life would resume to normal, two months and twenty-four days later, I receive a knock on the door from my dad telling me my brother died. Oh! my goodness! Lord, not again. This really hurts because I had planned on visiting him that morning. So now, once again, I was filled with grief and heartbroken. *This can't be real*, I thought, and again, I called on Jesus. "Lord, give me strength. I am depending on You." At that moment, I needed more and more of Jesus to help me stand.

My heart was still trying to mend. On November 6, 2009, I was in the courthouse, going through a divorce, which was filed on the same day my mother died. I thought, *What is wrong with me, Lord? Help me!* Personally, I think verbal abuse is worse than physical abuse. Words hurt and stay with you. When I was a kid, there was a saying "Sticks and stones break your bones, but words never hurt." Wow! I learned that's not true. I really needed a shoulder to lean on. I was both hurting and physically tired. Being married and getting saved didn't help, living unequally yoked. A believer and unbeliever won't make it. My husband looked at me with disgust and said, "I never want nothing to do with you ever again." I remember crying until my heart felt like it was going to explode, and suddenly, a voice said, "Pray." I tried praying, but all I could do was say, "Jesus! Have mercy. I can't do this on my own strength. I'm Your child. Please come see about me."

Even when we're going through hardships, we still must be able to listen when we pray because God answers. I have never hurt so much in my life.

Oh! By the way, God fixed that situation. My ex-husband and I are now the best of friends and he can't even understand why he does the things he does, BUT GOD!

On December 14, 2009, I became unemployed because the plant closed and moved to Mexico. So now, I needed a resolution to how my family and I were going to continue to make it. My mother was gone, my oldest brother was gone, my husband no longer wanted me, and my finances were in jeopardy. "Okay, Lord! Here I am! Casting all my cares on You. You said I have not because I ask not, and now I am putting everything in Your hands."

The months seemed to be getting longer. Depression was trying to take control, and the tears wouldn't stop. I was trying to do everything required of me as far as living right and being obedient. I was going to church every time the church door was open. I was praising God. I was fasting. I was calling on the name of Jesus, and the clouds were still hanging low. I realize that our timing is not God's timing and we have to be patient no matter what we go through, but when you're at your lowest, that is when the devil whispers the most, so you must stay "prayed up."

We all have a small amount of faith to believe something impossible and the Word of God says we only need faith the size of a mustard seed. The devil knows his time is near, so he is roaming around doing his job of stealing, killing, and destroying if we allow him to. I realize today that you can talk faith all you want, but there will come a time when you really must furnish that faith.

May 2010 brought on another test, and this one was personal. I was diagnosed with breast cancer, which literally knocked me off my feet. I cried like a river flowing, and I asked God, "Why me?" I have never had the Spirit speak to me so quickly, but the Spirit spoke back with the response, "Why not you?" I said, "Huh! Hmmm! I better leave this alone and move forward quickly." At this point, I thought about Job: and all his endurance and how God delivered and restored him. I know I serve a God who is mighty with all power in His hand and a God of no respector of person. Therefore, I believed that He was going to bring me through and I refused to give up.

Breast cancer is not easy to cope with on your own, and the hardest part about having breast cancer is the treatments of chemotherapy and radiation, and the side effects that you must live with. Even though I knew I was not alone, I felt alone because I wanted my mother, and that was impossible. I was the one going through this, but I had to be the strong one because my children were too weak to be of any comfort, and all I wanted was positive vibes and anything negative had to go. Outside of family, there was not much support, and the ones that said they would be there for me, weren't. God was my copilot, and I thank my pastor for being such a faith-teaching pastor, and that I accepted the Lord as my savior when I did. I owe God praise because I am still here surviving, and have been cancer free for the past seven years.

My battles did not seize. The stronger my faith got, the more things would come up. Some folks call me "shouting John" because I love to shout and praise God even when I don't feel like it. The devil didn't like that.

In August 2015, while doing routine housework, my knee snapped. Oh man! This was not good! A torn cartilage. I must have surgery. So now, the devil thinks he's got me. NOT SO! I can still use my hands and my mouth works. Hallelujah anyhow! Glory! I must be doing something right because the devil stays in my lane.

I refuse to give up! I am continuing to Praise God; praises going up and the blessings coming down. I knew that if God delivered me one time, He can deliver me again and again. In November 2015, a growth was discovered on my thyroid. After having a biopsy, I had to have surgery. I am blessed that I do not have to take thyroid medication for the rest of my life. God is so good! It's just amazing to me all the things that God does for me and I have never seen His face. Glory! I will tell the world that I love Him! I love Him! I love Him!

Getting blood work is something I must constantly do. During a routine check-up, something was spotted in my bloodstream, which required more intensive tests, such as pet-scan, cat-scan and MRI. In March 2016, another spot was spotted on my liver. I was back in the operating room without a clue as to what was really going on, except for the fact that I had a spot on my liver. Everybody was praying and fasting because of the risk involved.

After the surgery, the doctor was able to diagnose the condition as neuroendocrine tumor, a rare disease. I think the devil was trying to kill me, but God said NO! Not this time. At one point in my life, when I didn't know better and who I was serving, I would have given up, but knowing God for who He is and what He can do, giving up is not an option. I owe God praise for everything that He has brought me through in my life and without Him I am nothing.

On October 20, 2016, death visited us again and took my father. When I really think on all the death and how they occurred, I am not the one to question God for my reason for not being there when it happened. I would always wonder how

I felt about my father because as a child, we did not have a close relationship, but after the passing of my mother, God gave us another chance to reunite and make it right. I knew that living a godly life and being all God wanted me to be left no room for unforgiveness.

My life has not been easy, and the struggles have been real. Every time I think of them, I think of 2 Chronicles 20:15, which says *"This is what the Lord says to you: Do not be discouraged because of the vast army. For the battle is not yours, but God's."* I encourage anyone going through hardships to hold onto your faith no matter what it looks like, no matter what it feels like, and believe that though weeping may endure for a night, if you stand, joy will be there in the morning. There is nothing too hard or impossible that God cannot do. Ask yourself the question: Is there anything too hard for God? Just remember, when we are faced with the storms of life, we all need an anchor for our souls, so we do not destroy our lives. So hold on to hope, keep the faith, trust and believe, and always stand on the WORD OF GOD.

Realizing that life is predetermined, and nothing happens without God, made me recognize that through all my battles, I have gained strength to be an overcomer and to be victorious. Today, I am better, stronger, and wiser.

Linda C. Bush was born November 12, 1961 to the parents of Eva Devoe and George S. Creech. Linda is the eldest of four children, two deceased. Linda resides in Barnwell, South Carolina, where she attended and graduated from Barnwell High School. Linda is self employed and attends Colorado Christian University, previously pursuing a Bachelor's in Psychology. Linda's focus is to keep God first and everything good shall follow.

❧ ARNA EREGA ❧

Through Perseverance to Freedom

ARNA EREGA

Through Perseverance to Freedom

This is my short story of perseverance, love, passion, and leadership throughout my life events. I hope you find it encouraging and inspiring, and that you may see a new fire within you that will help you as you move forward toward your own goals and desires.

As a kid, I had so much energy my mother did not know what to do with me. So, she enrolled me in sports, and that was the best decision she ever made—I shall be eternally grateful to her for it. Because of my involvement in sports, my love for track and field grew bigger and fonder. By the age of twelve, I was training pretty seriously, and at fourteen, I made it to my very first World Youth Championships, where I did extraordinarily well. As the years passed, my times became faster, and I earned additional performances at World Youth and Junior Championships, European Championships, and European Youth Olympic Games. Soon, I was training like a professional athlete.

As I was growing up, I always hoped to come to the United States (US) to attend college and to pursue my athletic career and eventually be a professional track runner. Well, in 2007, I graduated high school, and admitted to several universities in the US. I chose a university in the Midwest. In August 2007, I packed my two big bags and came to the US on a full track and field scholarship. It was a dream come true. Or, so I thought!

My journey to the university was nothing even remotely close to what I had imagined. I chose this particular university because of the recruiting stories I was told before coming. The university, historically, had great athletes, and I was convinced that they had "the magic formula" to help me move on to the next level. Once I arrived there, I quickly gained about twenty pounds. Not long before, I battled an eating disorder, so it devastated me. Everyone had warned me before my departure, "Watch your weight! You will gain weight! Watch what you eat!" And, so I did. I watched what I ate; I even met with the nutritionist before all this weight started sticking with me. By December, I could not fit in any of my jeans, I was strong, my legs were huge, and as the indoor season kicked off, I was running slower than I ever did in my entire life! I was disappointed and heartbroken! During the spring semester, I slowly lost weight, but then I got mononucleosis. My athletic goal always was to make it to the Olympics—I missed the 2008 Beijing Olympics!

My remaining three years at the university, I was battling with the thought of transferring to another school, but then again I never considered quitting what I had started. So, I changed coaches in my junior year; I trained with the men's coach, and I trained on my own. That year, I ran a personal best of 13,44 seconds in 100 meter hurdles after three years.

Fast forward to my senior year—I was ready to get out of there! The environment was toxic, I had a physical fight with one of my teammates and ended up having seven stitches on my lip, and I was in a relationship for over three years with the man who was emotionally, verbally, and physically abusive toward me, but I loved him. Or, so I thought! My support was limited; the coaches did not care about my dreams, goals, and aspirations. They only cared whether I scored points at the conference meetings. I was eager to get my degree and move on. I used 2012 as an opportunity to get things in order and be in a positive environment; and try to get ready for the Olympic games in London during the summer.

I graduated in December 2011, and I moved to Columbia, South Carolina. I trained with a professional coach, who grew to be like a father figure. In February 2012, I fell at practice and broke my ankle. I did not know it was broken at that time; we just thought it was a severe sprain. I could not walk for over a month, and then I slowly started training again, but never changing my goal, never taking my eyes off the Olympic games. In June, I came home to run on the European circuit and continue to chase the Olympic standard. The qualification was 13.11 seconds, and I believe I ran 13.75 seconds that year up until that point. While I was in Europe, I was able to get an MRI in Croatia, which showed that a piece of bone chipped off in my ankle and its movement in my joint was damaging the cartilage tissue. I was unable to afford an MRI in the US when the accident occurred.

The doctors told me I have to have surgery if I wanted to continue to run and compete at the professional level. I told the doctor he would just have to wait after the Olympic games because I still had time to qualify and I could not have accepted the fact that I was going to miss yet another Olympic games due to some stupid injury! So, I ran. I ran several more races with the broken ankle. The pain was increasing and my time was not getting any faster. Thus, in the middle of July, I finally came to the realization I needed to schedule a date for the surgery.

During my stay in the US in 2012, I was on a temporary work permit (OPT) while still being on a student (F1) visa; I had a job as an after-school teacher at the private school. I was hoping to find a solution to be able to stay and work in the US. My visa was about to expire; I had no viable solutions. One option was to get back to school and pursue a master's degree. I wanted my master's in sports psychology, but there were no schools nearby offering that kind of program and moving was not an option at the time because it would mean having to change a coach. I searched for a program that was close and available and would still provide me with an opportunity to pursue what I wanted later on in life ultimately.

I started a Clinical Mental Health Counseling program in January 2013, which allowed me to renew my F1 visa. I was afraid I would have to leave the country because my visa would have expired, but everything was completed within the regulated time frame. As an international student, I was not allowed to work because my primary purpose of staying in the US was to attend school. International students are only allowed to work part-time on campus. At my school, there were no employment opportunities available. The tuition rates were ridiculous! In 2013 when I started, classes were $1,425; by the time I graduated in 2016, I was paying $1,745 per course. For someone coming from Croatia, where there is no minimum wage, and people work forty plus hours per week and only make $600 to $800 per month on average, those fees were out of reach. I could not have expected my parents to help me pay for school. The university did not have any assistantships available, and I could not have applied for financial aid because I am not a US citizen. Also, no bank wanted to give me a loan. Why? Well, because I am not a US citizen and no one wanted to co-sign for me. So, what did I do? I got my hustle on! No, I have never done anything degrading or illegal, but on several occasions, the thought of becoming a stripper crossed my mind. I persevered, and I believed that everything would work out as long as I did not give up. I worked five jobs—sixteen-hour days for three and one-half years with only three days off! I babysat for three different families. I did nails, by going to people's homes. I wrote other people's homework and research papers for money. I was even asked to write someone's dissertation! I declined that offer. I watched cats and dogs. I worked at the gym. I worked at the restaurant. I worked as a personal trainer. In addition to going to school full time, my internship was taking up to fifteen to twenty hours a week. My day would start at 4:30 a.m., and I would be ecstatic if I were in bed at 11:00 p.m. Ninety-hour weeks used to be nothing with no days off. Let me write it again, ninety hours per week for three and one-half years, and throughout that entire time, I had three days off, two Christmas days and the day I had my surgery to remove high-risk cancer cells off my cervix in 2015. I worked; I only spent my money on rent, gas, and utility bills, with the remaining going toward tuition. Three and one-half years, sixty credit hours added up to $45,000 with additional taxes and fees because I was an international student.

I graduated in October 2016. I obtained my temporary work permit (OPT) in December 2016, and I had secured a job with a company that promised to help me get the work (H1B) visa. Well, March came around, and the company suddenly decided not to pursue my H1B visa anymore. The deadline for work visa applications is always the first week of April. I missed the deadline; I resigned from that job due to lack of integrity on their part. I took and passed my licensure exam on April 8, becoming a licensed professional counselor. I spent two months searching for a job and finally obtained one at the end of May. Now, I just had a job that, even if they wanted to, could not help me to get a work visa. My work permit and current student visa was to expire in December. I was facing the same thing once again, but I chose to have faith and believe that in all things, God works for the good of those who love Him, who have been called according to His purpose.

In the last ten years, I have undergone numerous life changes, overcame an ankle surgery and possible development of cancer, paid for a master's degree out-of-pocket by working five jobs, while being unable to hold a real job. I have been an international student treated like an illegal immigrant, even though I obeyed the law and followed the rules. I have been forced to give up on my dream of making an Olympic team. I have been abused, lied to and cheated on by three different men. I endured an identity change from being an elite athlete to still trying to define myself in new terms.

Right now, I can only describe myself by five simple values. LOVE is the root of all things. INTEGRITY is a rare currency that is hard to come by these days. SACRIFICE is the price I must be willing to pay, no matter how high it may be, if I want to achieve the goals I have set for myself. COMMUNICATION makes everything easier. And, HONESTY is rare and difficult for most people.

Arna Erega is a native of Croatia, born in 1988. In 2007, Arna arrived in Nebraska to pursue her dream of becoming an Olympic athlete. Simultaneously, she pursued a degree in Psychology and Sociology at the University of Nebraska-Lincoln, which later led to an MA in Mental Health Counseling. Her professional running career was brief, but it taught her some invaluable lessons. Arna is now a licensed professional counselor (LPC-I) in the state of South Carolina. She is a member of American Counseling Association (ACA), South Carolina Counseling Association (SCCA), and South Carolina Counseling Association for Licensed Professional Counselors (SCALPC). Arna has also presented her research at the SCCA Annual Conference in 2016 and 2017 and at the SCALPC Conference in 2016. Arna's multilingual ability allows her to connect with people from all over the world. Her ability to plan and execute, in combination with her reliability, creativity, and attentiveness to detail, allowed her to achieve the status of scholar athlete, who is now aspiring to bring change and better lives to those around her in a positive direction one day at the time. Arna is founder and owner of Hurdling Through Life, LLC, a private counseling practice serving competitive individuals and professional athletes. Her passion is to help her clients overcome their fears and anxieties, create powerful relationships, and to use their own competitiveness throughout their journey of personal growth and development. Arna loves giving back to her community through various forms; she is involved in homeless outreach, has been a girl's track and field coach and mentor for several years now, and enjoys leading workshops pertaining to various topics, amongst many other things.

TAKILLA FLORENCE

Formed in the Womb

⇝ TAKILLA FLORENCE ⇜

Formed in the Womb

Before I formed you in the womb I knew you, before you were born I set you apart; I appointed you as a prophet to the nations.
—Jerimiah 1:5

As I watched my siblings sleep, I realized that this was not what "normal" life should be. It was

2:00 a.m., on a Tuesday night, and I was wide-awake, watching them sleep to make sure no rats bit them or that nothing crawled into their ears or mouths. I looked around at the boarded up windows.

I wanted to cry, but I couldn't; there was no more tears and, besides, crying would not change anything. So, I sucked it up. I was eleven years old when I understood I was "different."

My mother moved us to Waukegan, Illinois, to get away from everyone in order to start over. Or, that is what she told my grandmother that she needed to do. She said she wanted to "find herself." Instead, she found her friends, parties, and drugs, and lost her dignity and respect. While she was finding herself, I was losing myself.

I don't remember the exact day, but I do remember that we rode the Amtrak to Chicago in the spring. When we left Virginia, it was warm. When we arrived in Waukegan, after a thirty-seven-hour ride with three cranky kids, it was *freezing*! Mom's friend, Ethel, was waiting on us when we arrived. Though she was so excited to see my mother, she never once spoke to any of us kids. I knew at that moment, this was a bad idea. The plan was to stay with her until we could get a place of our own. How were we going to live with someone that didn't even want to speak to us?

We stayed with Ethel for two months, and it was two months of pure hell! She gave us *one* room to live in—one room with three active kids, my mother, whenever she was there, and me. One. Room. Filthy house, roach infested, all types of people coming and going all times of the night. Compared to what we "moved" into, it probably was a good deal. However, twice I had caught Ethel being mean to my sister. One day I came home from school and my brother told me that Ethel had come into the room and screamed at them because they were too loud. He was four years old. Two children confined to one room, for eight hours, while my other brother and I were in school, would create noise. When I asked her about what happened she cursed me out, an eleven-year-old, and told me that she would beat them with bats if she wanted to! I stood toe-to-toe with her and told her that if she ever hit either one of them I would be sure to call the police as soon as she had her next "party." That night she put us out. We moved up the block into a boarded up house, with no electricity, no heat, no refrigerator—*no nothing!*

Torn: To tear, rend, rip mean to pull apart. To tear is to split the fibers of something by pulling apart, usually so as to leave ragged or irregular edges.

I was so torn. Between being my mother's child and a good big sister and getting them out of this mess my mother had created. Trying to take care of three children, my mother and go to school all at the age of eleven had left me with ragged edges. I had always been loyal to my mother. I didn't want to see her in trouble. I didn't want the state to separate us. I didn't want to let anyone know that my mother made this big move and she still couldn't "find" herself. I tried everything in my power to "save" her. She would come home after being gone for days at a time, sometimes for a whole week. I would nourish her back while she told me all the things I had heard before, like, "Baby girl, I won't leave again" and "I am sorry" and "I am going to get myself clean" and "I can't do it without you" and the last one, "As soon as I get clean, we are going to be a happy family." That last one is the one I held on to the longest, wishing that it would come true.

So many things happened, things that probably should have broken me as a child. Once a month I had to make my brother go into the basement with me, which we called the dungeon, and put a penny in the electric box, just so that we could have electricity. I would steal groceries, although I really think the storeowner knew. He would always say, "Can you watch the front while I go to the bathroom?" and I never bought anything when he came back. I literally just laughed as I thought about it. I dug a hole in the backyard, put the cold stuff in a bag, and covered it so that it would stay cool because we didn't have a fridge. I had to go to the principal of my school and beg to be let out of school early because the guys on the corner would grab and touch and make horrible comments to me. If I had not changed my routine, I just knew they would rape and kill me. My biggest worry was if I died, who would take care of my siblings? I didn't even have enough sense to be worried about myself.

It was during the worst times that I remembered all the Sunday mornings my grandmother had dragged us to church, all her prayers, all the gospel songs she sung in the kitchen cooking Sunday dinners. Internally, I retreated to all those things. I would sing all of my grandmother's gospel songs to my siblings as I gave them baths. We would say our prayers together every night. After they would go to sleep, I would question God and ask him, "Why would You allow an innocent child to be born into such a hellish life?" and "Why would You allow such horrible things to happen to children?"

Someone told me that a man had been raping girls in the basement of our house. There was no more food and no way to get it. I hadn't had a full night's sleep in over six months and we hadn't seen my mother in almost two weeks. I knew, at that moment, I had to get us back to my grandmother.

After my mother had been gone for a month and we still didn't know where she was, my

grandmother had arranged for us to return to Virginia on the Greyhound bus. I spent two whole weeks

crying to my grandmother. I wanted to die. I felt like a failure. I felt like I had let my mother down. We still didn't know where she was; and she didn't know we had left Illinois. My mother knew some shady people in Illinois, so what if one of them had murdered her? It was during this time that my grandmother told me that I was a "special" child and that I was born for others. Back then, I had no clue what she meant.

Over the years, there were many, many hard situations. My mother finally surfaced from Chicago. We were given back to her numerous occasions and we were taken from her numerous times. We moved from state to state, from address to address, and from school to school. We were homeless at one point, and we were in foster care at another point.

As an adult, who has strengthened her relationship with God, I now know that all those hard things were necessary for me to become the woman that I am today. Those hard times taught me to pray, taught me to have faith, and taught me how to trust in the Lord because there were times when there was *no one else* to trust. Because of those tough situations, I learned to understand and help others who are going through difficulties in different stages of their life. Those tough times were paving the way for me to have empathy when dealing with life situations.

If I had never had those tough times, I would not have been prepared for the life that the Lord had planned for me. As a child, you don't know that tough times create tough people. You don't know to believe in yourself, but God knows; He knows who and what you are before you are even formed in the womb. He knew the obstacles that I would have to face. He knew the role that I would have to continue in my siblings' lives.

Our mother passed away ten years ago, and even through all those years, I still had to play the role of nurturing her right up until she was on her deathbed. I had to plan her funeral, shop for the clothes that she was buried in, and even pay for it, all while having to be there mentally and emotionally for my siblings. Before my mother slipped into a coma, her last words to me were, "Shawn (this is what my family calls me) take care of my kids." The Lord already knew the future and He had prepared me. In addition to caring for my siblings, I became a stepmother to six beautiful children, all of whom I love dearly. Had I not learned early on how to love someone else's children unconditionally, I would have never been able to be the mother to them that I have been. My destiny was formed in the womb.

For we are God's handiwork, created in Christ Jesus to do good works, which God prepared in advance for us to do.
—Ephesians 2:10

Takilla Florence is a visionary with a mind of a mogul and a heart of passion. Overcoming "dealt" life setbacks along with her own personal struggles, her story is one of achievement and proof that there is still hope in the world! She has overcome many obstacles to become an established entrepreneur, businesswoman and now published author. Takilla is the founder Divine Interventions, a support service that offers life coaching, consultation, mentorship, and motivational speaking. With over 20 years of blended family experience it is her life's journey to help and support others to embrace their peace and joy within their situation. Divine Interventions is home to the Mend the Blend™ movement. Through the Mend the Blend™ movement Takilla has been able to establish several programs that have benefited the blended family such as coaching services, support groups and so much more.

Takilla is living proof that determination, strength and faith will manifest your dreams. As a Certified Life Coach, mentor, motivational speaker and now author, it is her personal journey to motivate others to do the same. Takilla and her husband, James, have been married for over fifteen years and are the parents of six children, and have two beautiful grandchildren.

Takilla Florence is a Professional Certified Christian Life Coach through the New Life Coach Inc. To learn more, you can find her on Facebook at @interventions4u or call 940.268.5872.

KIMBERLY S. MIHALIK

Running Toward His Grace

⋙ KIMBERLY S. MIHALIK ⋘

Running Toward His Grace

"Rejoicing in hope, patient in tribulation,
continuing instant in prayer."
– Romans 12:12

I can't declare that I have always been the most tolerant in times of difficulty. Obstacles have always been present and continue to follow me like a meddling mosquito buzzing around my flesh. Often times, I struggle to be diligent with prayer and my spiritual life is lifeless like a cold, gray, winter's day in Michigan. In John 10:29, I find immense comfort: "*My Father, which gave them me, is greater than all; and no man is able to pluck them out of my Father's hand.*" *Phew!* What a relief that scripture brings me on those days I find myself aimlessly wandering through the twisted corn maze of life. Sometimes, it's like being stuck in a clip from the movie *Groundhog Day*. I am so thankful our King gives us a GPS for all the unplanned detours on our road trip of life!

If Jesus gave me some CliffsNotes in my early twenties about my life at forty-two, I would have choked on my Better Made BBQ chips and Dr Pepper from laughing so hard. Some of the titles I hold today are: nurse, mother, marathoner, health and wellness coach, triathlete, CPR instructor, wife, author, volunteer, board member, friend, and godmother. Christianity was not part of my childhood, nor was it present in my early adulthood. The Easter bunny and Santa Claus reigned at our humble abode and sadly, I never knew the Triune God until my late twenties. Navigating through the stormy sea of life as a youngster without the life jacket of scripture made my struggles seem like a tsunami at times. I felt like a duck helplessly trudging through a bad Exxon oil spill. Would I be stuck and covered in filth or washed clean with the waters of baptism?

My childhood left deep wounds and scars that contributed to overeating as an unhealthy coping mechanism. Although I have always enjoyed eating and still consider myself a 'foodie', there was a time that I had a very real food addiction that led me to a whopping two hundred seventy-one pounds. Food made me happy and I could eat an enormous amount of it without ever feeling full. I used food to dull my feelings from the tears I wept in nursing or from my unstable upbringing. Thankfully, through knowing my Savior, Jesus, the wounds and scars have healed and my craving for food is much more manageable. It is so much healthier to be full on His word rather than ice cream, cheeseburgers, and a side of Mountain Dew.

The unhealthy lifestyle followed me into my career as a nurse as I would indulge in my 3:00 a.m., vending snacks between code blues and unit disasters. Halfway through my career was when I first grasped onto what it was like to walk with the Lord. I have practiced medicine in some uber rad institutions and have seen God's handiwork firsthand. I have witnessed His children born into their temporary home and His flock led to their heavenly residence. The physical and mental strength of humans never ceased to amaze me. I have seen many earthly miracles in the OR, ER and ICU. It's practically a miracle that I went from morbidly obese to claiming victory on podiums in many races.

With Jesus' help, I have defied the odds and overpowered Satan's grip. I could have been a statistic, but the Lord had a plan for me. He does for all of mankind. God has blessed me with many talents, skills, and resources, some of which I never would have imagined just five years ago. I am using my gifts as a nurse, mom, athlete, and wellness coach to fuel the Kingdom. One of my all-time favorite sayings about how we treat our bodies is, "God created it, Jesus died for it, the Holy Spirit lives within it, so you had better take care of it." You were made in His image, so treating your vessel as the gem is honoring God.

Channeling the once negative emotions into the drive and motivation for a sport like triathlon has chiseled away the rough edges that have been nagging me for several decades. Self-discipline, determination, and mental grit are important attributes for anything in life, especially a sport like triathlon or a career as a nurse and mom. All the time, people ask me why I would want to subject my body to a grueling, demanding, and challenging sport that is heavily male dominated in my forties. Midlife crisis, maybe, which is a great guess! The answer is simple. It gives me time with Jesus and, in doing so, it keeps my body functioning well. The 4:00 a.m., wake ups, hours of swimming, biking, and running give me time to talk with God. I look to Him when I feel too weak to move another step. It is my scheduled time to be grateful for all He has done for me and meditate on his Holy Word. Training gives me an opportunity to pray and appreciate God's marvelous creations all around me. It is like a personal training session with the Lord.

Whatever you're doing in life, if you have passion and seek the Lord in your quest, Satan can't mislead you so easily into negative coping mechanisms. Satan knew my weaknesses and played them like a seasoned actor during a play. This wasn't the theatre, however, and I wasn't an actress—this was my life. If I kept treating my body like a trash can, I would be at the bottom of the heap, slowly rotting away and missing life's beautiful moments. I often ponder about all the moments with my children and husband that would not be feasible if I didn't take charge of my choices. Glory to God in the highest for maintaining my health throughout the battle that raged within me. Not having any chronic illnesses that I could have developed being that obese is a blessing.

All the attributes it takes to be a "great anything" in life comes with a hefty price tag of sacrifice. Life is too short and amazing to be mediocre. Every exhausting twelve to sixteen-hour midnight shift in the ICU has shaped me as an athlete, mom, wife, and friend. It taught me to work tirelessly and not give up until God was ready to take that person away from the earth. Every tear shed and frustrating moment in my career helped mold my endurance in whatever task was at hand. I think of Romans 5:3-4: *"And not only so, but we glory in tribulations also: knowing that tribulation worketh patience; and patience, experience; and experience, hope."* Experiences, whether good or bad, are powerful tools that shape and mold you as a sister or brother in Christ. Sometimes, we don't realize the trials we face today are strengthening us for the adversity we may encounter days, months, or even years later.

I finally figured out the connection of body, mind, and spirit and it was like a rocket blasting off into the heavenly skies. I felt like I finally had a good outer rim of the puzzle of life pieced together. Empowered by what I discovered, I prayed about how to get my earthly body healthy. To my surprise, He answered my prayer very quickly. I adore the Smoky Mountains, and it is a special place for my family and me. My second son is even named after a portion of it—Cade's Cove. Almost four years ago, I stumbled upon a Facebook post about an inaugural half marathon in the Smoky Mountains. I was very intrigued by the race location, but I also knew it would be very difficult with the hilly terrain. So, I kept praying and armed with the confidence of the Holy Spirit, I entered the lottery for a free entry. At the time, I was just shy of two hundred sixty pounds and had only run a 5K. I also knew the likelihood of winning a free entry was a long shot because I never "win anything." Well, Jesus made sure I knew He heard my prayers loud and clear because *bam!* I WON! It was very daunting, visualizing the strategy to execute my goal of finishing. Armed with a vision, faith, and a book, I began to train my very large unconditioned body to do things it had never done before. There were many tears, lots of ice baths and, many times, I questioned my sanity. I had to do tons of self-affirmation. If I could work in a stressful nursing environment, save lives, and bear children from my imperfect body, I knew I surely could cross that finish line with God's help. I was diligent and faithful with my training. I stayed honest with my expectations and continued to chip away at the nagging baggage that held me hostage in my own body for so long. Six months later and about forty pounds lighter, I found myself at the start line of the Inaugural Smoky Mountain Half Marathon. I was, by far, the biggest person out there in spandex. Compared to others, I felt like an Italian sausage, bursting out of its casing. I was hovering around two hundred twenty pounds the day I CROSSED THAT FINISH LINE!

What I learned about myself on that hot, humid September morning in 2014 helped mold me into the determined Christian I am today. I also discovered the incredible support of the running community. I had so many athletes cheer me on and encourage me along the way. I discovered the triathlon world next and the supportive nature of other athletes defying the odds was like a comfortable church on a Sunday morning. The rest, like my weight, is history. I did not rely on gimmicks, fads, or surgery, but rather used dedication, perseverance and prayer to change my lifestyle. One half marathon led to another and, as I continued to slay my goals, my dreams got bigger. I can say that God has kept me injury free for five half marathons, one full marathon, thirteen sprint triathlons, one Olympic distance triathlon and soon to be my first half Ironman that consists of a 1.2-mile swim, fifty-six-mile bike and a 13.1-mile run, totaling 70.3 miles. Roadblocks are still present as I train, but now I am equipped and trained to use the same tools and techniques God has given me to be successful throughout my journey in life.

My next goal is to cross the finish line at a full Ironman and God willing, that will happen soon. My preparation and perseverance to arrive at the starting line is the achievement; the race itself is just a celebration of my journey. My experiences as a mother, wife, nurse, and athlete have given me so much fuel to blaze full throttle through this blessed and chaotic life I lead. My chapters are ever changing and I continue to marvel at how the Lord intervenes in my life. I will never be an Olympian, but rather a weekend warrior who still loves her BBQ potato chips. Learning to cope in other ways loosened Satan's grip. Jesus died on the cross for me and I was baptized into His kingdom to one day be reunited with Him in paradise. Knowing, believing, and spreading that joyous news helps me become the person God created me to be.

Be patient, my fellow sisters in Christ; know and trust that God has a plan for you. In whatever season you are in, ride the route of uncertainty with powerful reminders in scripture, knowing He will guide and mold your life. Equip yourself with scripture wherever you are in life and go confident, spreading the word of the Lord amongst the earth. Shalom!

Kimberly Mihalik calls southwest Michigan her home. The one unique thing Michiganders get to do is use their hands as maps. Look at your right hand and her stomping grounds are just about where the meaty part of your left lower pad meets your wrist bone. Her husband Scott has shared in Kimberly's life's joyous adventures for thirteen years. Two boys named Mikhail and Caiden call her mom and make sure they keep her on her toes. Sheena is her faithful training partner, part Beagle and part Shepherd, and is always eager to help with her mom's fitness endeavors. When Kimberly isn't busy being a mom, wellness coach, wife, nurse, teaching CPR, training or volunteering at her church, travel is her passion. Before marrying the love of her life, she planned to work as a travel nurse around the USA, appreciating its striking beauty. Thirteen years later, as well as eight moves, four cities, two kids and a dog, that dream has been replaced with taking advantage of what the Mitten state (Michigan) has to offer when it's not like the arctic tundra or getting swarmed by ticks and skeeters. Living by Lake Michigan comes with its quirkiness of having all four seasons sometimes in one week and a plague-like amount of bugs. The weather is unpredictable and makes you be prepared and endure the ever-changing conditions like life. I should have given credit to my home state for making my perseverance what it is today! Cruising in an RV, while exploring God's creations, is the alternate travel goal to the original travel nurse vision. Being a board member of the Michigan Alliance for Prevention of Sudden Cardiac Death of the Young allows her to spread information regarding sudden cardiac death. The alliance is a statewide collaborative network that strives to encourage communities to be prepared in a sudden cardiac arrest. When not being a weekend warrior in the running and triathlon world, cooking, and reading, spending time with family and being an electronic hoarder on Pinterest is valued and enjoyed. Need coaching or want to stay in touch? Head over to www.bellaADHDcoaching.com and follow her on Facebook.

L'TARRA MOORE

There is More

There is More

After many years of playing it safe and only doing things she was comfortable with, there came a time in Sydni's life where she felt there was something else she needed to do. Sydni was the CEO of a large advertising firm. She and her business were extremely successful and known all over the world. Over the years, Sydni and her company accumulated awards and significant recognition for their work. It did not matter how accomplished Sydni was; there was a continuous nudging Sydni kept getting that gave her the idea that there was something else to do.

Has this ever happened to you? When you were in a right stable place, where you had something to show for all your hard work, accomplishment after accomplishment and you still felt like there was something else. After college and getting her career off the ground, for years, Sydni worked and worked hard. She struggled and sometimes struggled hard. She pushed and pushed until she made it. But, there was something else. Even though she was overjoyed and proud of her achievements, that notion she kept getting made her feel that she had not yet reached fulfillment and that made her uncomfortable. It was as if life were saying, "You have one more thing to do." Isn't that how it always is? You look at your life and know that you have done well, accolades were given to you because of your skills, and you know you are almost there, almost at a point where you were fulfilled. When you can exhale, smile and you are right there at a peak in your career where you could say I have made my mark in this world. Then, in your quiet time, when your feet are up, and you are slightly laid back in your chair, you feel a poke, push, or an uncomfortableness that makes you move. That makes you say, "What is that?"

Throughout her career, Sydni has always wanted to establish a school for the youth that would encourage by teaching confidence in different ways. It would also educate and train the youth on other subjects and technology. Sydni's desire was for the students to go into the world believing they could do anything and were well rounded. She had a strong desire to start this school. She was also very hesitant because she did not know where to start. When the first thought came, Sydni was just building her advertising firm, so she kept working on her firm until the strong urge came back to the school for youth. Sydni began to write down what she wanted the school to offer and the location of the school. She would fantasize about the youth attending her school and the youth learning. As business picked up for her, the busier she became. Sydni felt like maybe this is what she was supposed to be focusing on and not her dream of a school. Sounds familiar? You start one thing and also have a vision of something entirely different. Sometimes, what you envision is stronger than what you are skilled to do. Sydni has always had a passion for going over and beyond showing her appreciation for others, especially those who invested in her life. She thought about where she came from and always wanted to do something back home because that was her foundation. Sydni would sit and think about how she could say, "You poured into my life. All the discipline, love, support, and every conversation that helped to build me to who I am today."

After years and years of building her advertising firm to one of the most successful companies, Sydni finally decided it was time to work on her longtime dream. She knew she was going to need help with building her school. After much prayer, she called on a few people she knew she could trust with her vision and her feelings. She knew that in this process, she would have to have people working with her she could be honest with and say, "I do not know what I am doing, building and starting a school, but I know, without a doubt, that I have to do it." It was important that the select few also believed in her vision for the school and they had to understand her passion for wanting to build the school. The select few she chose worked hard to help Sydni. Every step of the way, every hurdle they were there. She needed this group to be there with her. They were her cheering corner, her wise counsel, and prayer partners. She needed them! This was something else Sydni was experiencing, that was new to her. She had to rely on a person with something that was so valuable to her. In one of their meetings, Sydni confessed, "All these years, I have been so careful, doing what I knew better than anything else and now, I am in unfamiliar territory." Sydni said, "Y'all, I am scared!" The only thing that kept Sydni pushing forward was knowing someone took a chance on her, sacrificed for her and now she had to take a chance on someone, even if that meant taking one of the most significant risks in her life.

Sydni retired her advertising firm and has a full-time staff heading her school. Now, she can sit back with ease. One of her staff members brought her a write up from a magazine. The article talked about Sydni and her success, and this statement was made: "Stepping out on faith, Sydni would set the world on fire by supporting their future with education and confidence." She responded to the statement saying, "Sending young people out into the world with confidence, knowledge, and skills would be a great way to say, 'THANK YOU and I APPRECIATE WHAT YOU DID FOR ME,' to those who took that chance on me when I was younger." As Sydni read each sentence, she came across, "Sydni Arlington, African American women, founder of one of the largest advertising firm…" Sydni chuckled and said, "As proud as I am to be an African American woman. I do not want the color of my skin to be the leading, describing adjective of who I am." Sydni went on to say, "I want to be defined as a Christian woman who stepped out on faith and did her part in this world." For Sydni, it was more important for people to know that she had faith, she used her faith, and whatever they want to do, it can be done as long as they step out on their faith and believe. Whatever you want to do, it can be done as long as you have faith and you step out on it. You can do anything. Do not ignore that dream, that push, that desire or that nudge. It means there is more for you to do. And remember, whoever is watching you just maybe inspired by your faith that helped you to recognize that there is more.

L'Tarra Moore is the daughter of Pastor George Moore (deceased) and Mrs. NettieLewis Moore. She taught Basic Computers to three to four year olds at Saint Philip Child Development Center for ten years. She is now working on the Marketing Team at Saint Philip A.M.E. Church. She loves to encourage and help people. L'Tarra has many talents such as photography, singing, cooking and baking. She is a lover of music and enjoys a great movie and/or television show. She is now continuing her education in the technical field and her new venture is writing.

JENNIFER RODRIGUEZ

Piece by Piece

JENNIFER RODRIGUEZ

Piece by Piece

"O Lord my God, I cried unto thee, and thou hast healed me. O Lord, thou hast brought up my soul from the grave: thou hast kept me alive, that I should not go down the pit."

—Psalm 30:2-3

April 7, 2011, was the day that forever changed my life. It was on this day that I was placed under arrest and booked into the Lea County Detention Center for driving under the influence. As intoxicated as I was, I can still vividly remember that jail cell and being so overwhelmed by feelings of shame, humiliation, guilt, and complete desperation. I wasn't always like this, an out of control alcoholic. In fact, in the years past, I was the furthest thing from it. Yes, I went through some rebellious years as a teen, but in February 1998, at the age of twenty-two, I made the decision to give my life to God. Immediately following my born-again experience, I immersed myself in the church and attended services every time the doors were open. Shortly after getting saved, I met my future husband in church and, after nine months of dating, we got married, and served in the church as youth leaders. Two years later, we welcomed our first daughter, followed by our second daughter three and a half years later. We had a seemingly perfect life and were blessed beyond our dreams. In 2003, while studying the Word of God, I distinctively heard God speak to me. He said, "Jennifer, I have called you to minister. I want you to prepare a sermon." In my astonishment, yet excitement, I shared this revelation with my pastor, who was even more thrilled than me. He offered me a day to preach and so began my ministry. I preached at the pulpit when offered and led other various programs within our church. I felt a great sense of pride and accomplishment.

In November 2005, my mother passed away at the age of fifty-one. Her unexpected death turned my world upside down. For the first time in my life, I experienced the pain of grief. My mom was my best friend. I can't even put into words how much her death completely devastated me. I had lost all enthusiasm and interest in preaching and teaching. My family and I still attended church, but I became increasingly numb and unresponsive toward God. I continued to preach on a few occasions, but not with any kind of excitement. And within a year, and without a word, I had withdrawn from ministry altogether. I grew content just showing up on Sunday mornings, if I managed to do that.

Eventually, I got bored with life and decided to go to cosmetology school. It seemed like a good idea at the time, but looking back, I now realize it was just something to fill the void I had created when I lost connection with God. It was nearing the end of the two-year cosmetology program when I started to drink heavily. I had a few large projects to finish up before graduating the program, I was under a lot of pressure, and drinking seemed to take the edge off. My alcohol consumption started off, like any addiction really, just a little here, a little there. But, within a matter of weeks, I was drinking more and more. I drank liberally at home and even during school hours. My alcohol consumption and behavior quickly spiraled out of control. I somehow managed to complete school, but my drinking didn't stop there, it only got worse. My family and friends took notice and expressed concern, but I was hooked—mentally, emotionally, and physically. My husband tried to make sense of my downward change. He scheduled appointments with a few psychiatric doctors for me, hoping they could help me. But, at that time, neither doctors nor the medicines they prescribed could save me from the allure of alcohol. As I continued to drink, my behavior became exceedingly erratic and dangerous. On more than one occasion, my husband had to call the police to our home to take control of my drunken and irrational conduct, which usually landed me in an emergency room. And, in due course, I had gotten myself admitted into two different psychiatric wards. At this point, my relationship with God was pretty much nonexistent. Consumed with immense shame and guilt, I avoided all contact with God, terrified of what He might say to me.

On November 2010, extremely intoxicated and overcome with desperation, I took handfuls of prescription pills in an attempt to end my life. But, by the grace of God, my husband came home only minutes later to discover what I had done and called 911. I don't remember much about this emergency room visit, as I was in and out of consciousness. By a miracle, I survived. The following day, the doctor informed me that he was having me involuntarily admitted to a psychiatric hospital. I begged my husband to do something, anything to get me out of having to go to another psych ward, but he refused. He had hopes that my stay there would get me the help I obviously needed. During my seven-day stint in the psych ward, I met with a psychiatric doctor, which recommended I go to inpatient treatment for addiction. The thought of going to rehab terrified me. I felt that after being locked up in a psychiatric hospital for seven days, I had learned my lesson. I was determined to get sober after that experience and made promises to myself and to my loved ones that I would do better and be better.

After being discharged from the psychiatric hospital and armed with only my self-will, I managed to pull off a few weeks of sobriety, but before long, I was back to my old drinking habits and the chaos my addiction caused within my family soon followed. My husband was at his wits end and my children were in a state of confusion and fear. My old foes, shame, regret, and desperation soon returned with a vengeance, but even with all the turmoil, I could not make myself get or stay sober.

Then on April 7, 2011, after my arrest on DWI charges and placed in a "drunk tank," I finally broke. Overcome with embarrassment and remorse, I questioned how I let myself get to this point. Here I was—a so-called woman of God who had preached and taught others the Word of God, a wife, a mother—now locked up in a jail cell with nothing but my shame. I had nowhere to go and no one to call for help, so I did the only thing I could do…I cried out to God for the first time in over a year. The following day was to be my arraignment, but I was informed that morning that the judge would not be in court that day. I was told that unless someone came to bail me out, I would have to wait five more days, in jail, until the judge was back in court. I knew no one was coming to bail me out, everyone I knew thought I was exactly where I needed to be. I felt utterly helpless and hopeless. Although I knew I deserved to be in jail, I pleaded with God, and told Him that if He made a way for me to get out, that I would seek help…real help. Long story short, I managed to bail myself out. My husband was not real pleased, but I assured him I was committed to getting help, even if that meant going to rehab. The day I was released from jail, our church was hosting a women's conference and, with all my guilt and all my shame, I went to the conference that night. The women, who knew of my circumstances, comforted and loved on me. I was so overwhelmed by the love God poured on me over the course of that conference. I was still struggling with feelings of disgrace, but because I reached out to God, He reached down to me.

Keeping up with my end of the bargain, when the conference ended, I sought treatment. I researched Christian women's treatment facilities and was immediately drawn to one in particular. Although anxious about making the decision to go treatment, I called my husband to tell him about this rehab. I explained to him that I felt a peculiar peace about this place, and that I would have to commit to thirty days of inpatient treatment. We prayed about it and we both agreed this place was where I was meant to go.

Three days later, I arrived at the treatment center, anxious and scared. Yet, soon after arriving, I felt more relaxed and at peace with my decision. I met women there, who, just like me, were wives, mothers, and fellow Christians who had lost their way and were recovering from the grips of addiction. In time, I heard about their personal struggles with addiction, and the details of their stories. I soon learned about how their addictions triggered destructive behavior similar to mine. For the first time in over a year, I didn't feel so alone. I felt understood and accepted. A sense of hope started to ignite within my spirit. I knew then God had indeed not forsaken me. While there, with complete honesty and consistence, I sought God in prayer and truly committed to the recovery process.

There are no sufficient words to describe the overpowering love and peace that began to flood my entire being. The first couple weeks, I learned a lot about addiction and the effects it has on one's mind and body. Through my restored relationship with God, He taught me how to forgive myself and to accept His merciful forgiveness. Yet, still, an even more surprising change was in store. God revealed to me the many false beliefs I had about Him that ultimately led to my downfall. I was not only in treatment for my addiction, but that He guided me there for something much more miraculous.

God showed me how my inaccurate, preconceived opinions about Him had affected my relationship with Him. Before my stay in treatment, it had been years since I experienced the unconditional love of God. Therefore, my judgments of Him were beliefs of condemnation and punishments. Quite honestly, after years of living with these notions about God, this new revelation confused me and a million questions surfaced in my mind. If God didn't want to punish me, then what did He want to do with me? What did He want me to believe about Him? How else was I to perceive Him? In time, the answers emerged. God wanted nothing more of me than to accurately believe that He is good, that He loves me unconditionally, and that He desires for me to be whole, to be at peace in mind and spirit. God wanted me to completely change my perspective of who I believed Him to be. During a counseling session with my husband, he made an extremely profound statement that is forever etched in my spirit. He explained it like this: "You have been viewing God as if He were an old, black and white TV, when in reality, God is more like a high-definition television, vivid and full of color." I realized then I had put God in a box labeled a "cruel and disapproving Father." God confirmed to me that it was time to see Him, for who He really is, a loving, faithful, forgiving, merciful God who is on my side, who is for me and not against me. Even though I was experiencing a transformation, it took some time for me to process the new perception of God.

The day I completed treatment, I felt born-again, yet apprehensive, too. I feared falling back into old thinking habits and failing at recovery and I had to concentrate on a new and unfamiliar relationship with God. So, for the year that followed treatment, I focused all my attention on my recovery and my brand-new connection with God. There were days I felt lost and perplexed. I questioned if grasping God in this new light was really how He wanted me to comprehend Him. With time and a continual connection with God, I was able to receive God for His true nature, LOVE! God took my brokenness and pieced me back together, piece by piece, with patience and His perfect love.

Today, I experience God's love everywhere. I'm completely surrounded by it. It's in my connection with Him, with my amazing husband, with my two awe-inspiring daughters, and a host of remarkable friends and family. I share my story with you not only in hopes to encourage you, but also because I believe it was in God's divine plan. It has been through this crazy journey of mine that I have discovered God's plan and purposes for my life—to help others who are suffering from hopelessness, to express God's love to them, so they, too, will discover all that God has planned for them. Perhaps our stories are different, but maybe you can relate to the depressing feelings of shame, brokenness, and desperation. Perhaps you've done what I did and put God in a box and falsely labeled it as "cruel and condemning Father." Let me reassure you, God loves you unconditionally. God desires for you to be whole and to be at peace with yourself and with Him. God longs for a connection with you. You're not damaged beyond repair or worthless to Him. God can take your brokenness and piece you back together, better and stronger than you've ever been. God can and will rescue, redeem, and restore you, because He has purpose for you, an extraordinary destiny that is beyond your wildest dreams.

"Who hath saved us, and called us with an holy calling, not according to our works, but according to his own purpose and grace, which was given us in Christ Jesus before the world began."

—2 Timothy 1:9

Jennifer Rodriguez is wife to Trini for eighteen years and mom of two daughters: Zion and Aubri Joi. She is involved in leadership at New Hope Ministries as a core team member and leader of the NHM Connections Team. She is also a soon-to-be certified Christian Life Coach through New Life Coach Inc. Jennifer's passion is connecting with the hearts of women through sharing her story of God's restoration, love, and hope.

⁂ LORETTA SCOTT ⁂

A Mother's Silent Cry

LORETTA SCOTT

A Mother's Silent Cry

I grasped my chest, trying to hold back the tears from falling. Hoping that gripping my chest would somehow soothe the pain in my heart. It was way too intense, and my left arm weakened, losing tenacity and strength. Was this a stroke? As I climbed the stairs in slow motion, reaching the top seemed forever, a task I was so used to doing like a hop and skip; I was physically fit and on active duty status. I was stationed at Walter Reed Hospital in the District of Columbia and resided in Maryland alone. I did not have any immediate family here; they were all in other states. I had to report to duty in a few hours, but the news I received was too overwhelming for me to ponder anything else. The call came at three in the morning, awakening me as I had fallen asleep on the couch. It was my daughter calling to inform me my youngest son was in jail, locked up, a number, another Black man's dream deferred, interrupted by a system with no empathy for him.

Unable to wrap my head around what had transpired, I was surprised, felt helpless without hope, and alone. I was a mother first, and this mother's love was real, taking control of every emotion I possessed. I was crying, and could not fathom the idea of my son, my child, my youngest held in a county jail. *It cannot be real*, I tried to tell myself, but it was real, just as real as the pains coursing through me. As a nurse, I knew I had a stroke. I had experienced all the symptoms. I found myself on the floor, and I crawled to the phone and called my eldest son, who was consoling, but not enough to erase my pain or to make this all go away. Yes, I wanted to go to sleep and to wake up knowing this nightmare would all be gone, cast away in the dark sea of hell. What I desired and what happened was not going away. *I have to pull myself together, and allow God to take center stage.*

I lay on my bed, feeling numb, but I knew I had one thing left to do. I had to call on the name of Jesus. I cried out to the Father in Heaven that He would hear my cry, and send me the Comforter because, even in my craziness of denial, I knew this was bigger than I was. As I called on God, tears began to flow more, and my heartache became less painful. I tried to rationalize my son's behavior, tried to understand what happened to cause this. I knew I was a good mother; I had college degrees, I love the Lord, I raised them in the church, I treated people with respect and dignity, I made sure they lived in lovely homes, my children never wanted for anything. Between talking to God and feeling sorry for my son and myself, I had to sleep; I had to be to work in a few hours. I let out a loud scream and held onto my chest, and continued to pray to the Lord; He was my only hope, I needed to depend on Him.

Morning came too fast, and my eyes were puffy from crying, but I had to work. I hurried into the bathroom to put a hot cloth over my eyes, taking turns from right to left in hopes the puffiness would decrease. Being active duty and calling in sick was more difficult than the civilian world. When a person is sick on active duty, they report to "sick call" and then they are told if the soldier will get quarters, medicines, or both by the doctor. Calling in sick was not an option. I needed to work to keep my weary mind busy. I prayed before I left home and in the car, while

I drove. I managed to stay upbeat until I realized I had to find a lawyer for my son. It was difficult because I was in a different state alone with no one I could share this burden with other than God. I found a lawyer, called him, left my name and waited until he called me back. In the meantime, my daughter was able to bail my son out with the transferring of money, and he was able to meet with the lawyer regarding his case.

After a few days, my son had his first hearing. I was a basket case, I could not eat, and I poured myself into cleaning, and doing everything else to keep my thoughts off my son while waiting to hear from the lawyer with the consequences. These few days were breathtaking. I talked to my son and he showed remorse for what he did, and took full responsibility for his actions. I was at work when I was summoned I had a phone call. It was the lawyer, with good news and bad news. I was not prepared to hear any bad news; I just could not take any more, it was way too much to bear by myself. The lawyer said my son was facing fiffteen years, and he was doing everything in his power to get a new judge, but the young Black prosecutor requested this, and he refused to back down or change the sentence. I could not believe the prosecutor. This was my son's first offense, but drug and gun charges did not make it better. Oh, how I prayed. I was also a wounded woman with silent cries. I knew much too often about the silent cries that I have grown accustomed to doing every so often. It is not easy being a mother, especially when you are raising your children alone. You are already feeling the guilt with the absent father. These feelings have a way of suffocating the right things a mother does, such as nourishing, and the love she gives.

One day, while sitting at home, I decided to call my favorite aunt to pray for her since she was going through some changes. While I was praying for her, I visualized the jail, and just as my son walked through the closing gate, a white eagle flew in. I was in awe, but I knew the power of the Holy Spirit and God's work. Despite the visual, my heart felt so heavy, and I could not understand and shake the fact that my son might be away from the family and me for fifteen years; I would not see him again until he gets out. Only because I always told my children if they ever get in trouble, I will help them with good counsel, but I cannot do jails or prisons. I needed God more than ever. The heartache of losing my child for fifteen years was too intense, and my mind was racing with all sorts of negative thoughts.

The next day I received a call from the lawyer, once again while at work, I hesitated to answer, and I could almost feel as if my heart was leaping out of my chest. The lawyer this time informed me of the removal of the young, Black prosecutor from the case, and they have a new person he can negotiate. My son was detained and to stay in jail after his court date. The lawyer said if I could get a job lined up, and pay the owner weekly, my son could escape jail and do some probation, but he would not have a felony on his record. I agreed to the terms. Later that night, I was feeling overwhelmed and as I was walking upstairs, I was crying and praying for my son. Then, God stopped me and asked, "Why are you crying?"

"Because my son must stay in jail," I said.

God said, "But he was facing fifteen years."

He was right, I was crying, and my son was being released in two days and did not serve but seven days in jail.

As mothers, we are often placed in positions where we must defend our children and are weakened by the things they do. We cry in silence, we hurt, because we feel helpless and hopeless, but if we remember to put our faith in God, nothing is impossible. God can move mountains; He can make the crooked road straight, and move people out of our way. We must continue to call on Him in times of need and never feel you are alone. Our children have no clue what a mother does. They don't see the tears we cry while they are asleep, or the worries of trying to make ends meet. Or the hesitation, and the thumping heartbeats, and pain our heart feels when the phone rings after the midnight hour. The silent cry of a mother is real, but if we hold fast onto God's unchanging hand, He will guide us, direct our paths, and prove to us He is who He says He is.

Mothers are notorious for blaming themselves for the choices their children make. When you have done all you can do and have made the environment safe for your child or children; you should never feel guilty. Many mothers do blame themselves, thinking they may have missed something or they did not give enough. The real truth is mothers provide too much, and often neglect themselves, and get little back in return.

I am grateful God kept my son and, despite the times I became weary, He still watched over me, protected me, and directed my path. Sometimes, life throws us curve balls and we must be able to discern them and put our trust in God. All we need is a mustard seed, which is not much. I'm better today; I don't panic when phone calls come in the wee hours. I try to allow God to direct my journey because He already knows the outcome. Who would have thought that my son was facing more than half his age for his first offense? Fifteen years is a long time, and God only allowed seven days, and seven in God's world is consider completion. No one could have prepared me for this, but I knew the Lord, and through my constant prayers, He was able to do the impossible.

My son is in the right place now. I think these stumbling blocks have made him a restored young man, and yes, he still has a lot to learn. When we pray, we must believe God will do what we ask, and wait until God moves on our behalf. We must leave our troubles with God and allow God to fight our battles.

We will have all types of battles and obstacles that may come our way, but one must never feel defeated at what they want to achieve, and what they want God to do in one's life. Sometimes, it feels like God is not moving fast enough, and the enemy wants us to believe that it is useless to wait on God, but I speak from experience. *Wait*, be of good encouragement, and obedient to know God is who He said He is and will do what He said He would do. I understand that life is not always fair, and curve balls will come, and they will come, but I assure you, if you believe that God will show up and show out, then allow the curve balls to come, because His Blood already covers you. I say follow your dreams, the set-backs, and the interruptions because as long as you're living, these obstacles will come. Allow yourself to learn, and walk in your destiny, trusting your ability that you can and knowing you are serving a Higher power. It is my wish that you trust God, tell Him what you need and desire and hold fast unto Him, no matter what it looks like, and know that in the end you will see your miracle.

Loretta Scott is a published author of "Yes I Can, an Army Nurse story before, during, and after Desert Storm. She is retired from the military as an Army Nurse. She resides in the state of Maryland. She remains active as a nurse, and believer in Christ. She has three beautiful children who live in other states, with one son retired from the Army. She is a proud grandmother of five grandsons. Previously, she has published with the Women Compilation Project. Currently, she is working on several books soon to be published. God's Speed.

TRACEY L. SIGERS

Confessions of a Beauty Queen

"Design Essentials"

TRACEY L. SIGERS

Confessions of a Beauty Queen

"Design Essentials"

When I look into the mirror, what do I see? I see everything You created me to be. I see You made me in Your image tried and true, and You, God, gave me spiritual garments that look like You. But, in my walk, I have found that there are those who want me to wear the garments they choose. The garments are beautiful and I like them, too, but what I realized is when I put them on, I no longer look like You.

This is Confessions of a Beauty Queen.

While growing up in the eighties, it was hard for me to embrace who I was. I grew up in a season of *if you are light you are all right and if you are dark, well you have a few problems.* Even after winning the Ms. Black Ohio title, I was somewhat confident, but I used that garment of confidence to cover up a lot of hurt and pain. Called the ugliest girl in high school had set the stage for me to clothe myself in images that were not the images God had designed for me.

I was a young adult in my early twenties when I was having a conversation with a friend one day. I was telling her about a guy who I was interested in. Of course, I was excited and really wanted to make sure I did everything right so I could get to know him better. We started dating and having a great time. I would share my dating experiences with my friend (this is where I went wrong), thinking she would be excited for me. During one conversation, I asked her, "Don't you think he is cute?" and she replied, "He is cute enough for you." Yes, you read correctly. I was so taken aback by her comment, I wanted to act like I did not know what she was saying, but I did; I knew exactly what she meant.

What I would soon later realize in life is that some people don't want you to have what they don't have or what they cannot get for themselves. My friend's comment did not stop me from dating the guy, but what it did do was create another pathway for the devil to come in and make me doubt myself. Because of my strength, I realized the devil had to come down every avenue of my life to try to tear me down. He could not do it with drugs or drinking, so he did it with words. The very gift of writing and speaking that God gave me, the devil used it against me.

I thought I was quite confident in my image…or was I? I found that although I knew I was good enough, I still wanted to try to fix or change the image that God had for me. Words had worked their way into my image closet and assisted me in choosing my life garments. Although we do not realize it, those image changes can come through makeup, clothes, attitudes, and people with whom you associate. Often, I found myself using tools of the world to change my image. I loved fashion so I embraced it, not realizing that those garments were just a cover up. Even in changing your own garments, people will still have an opinion of what those garments should look like on you. People can dress up and be "Sugar Sharp," but still be a mess on the inside. I realized that was me and I had not accepted the skin I was in. A writer once said, "People with a purpose are happy people and live longer because they have a future to look forward to." I did not know my purpose and, thus, could not see my future. What a scary place to be in. I was in that scary place.

Once I stopped letting people define me and dress me in their image with their words, I started to realize what my image should look like. I left the scary and the unknown and started loving me. Garments that God has for me are designed for me and they come to me hot off the "streets of gold runway" designed for my purpose. My image garments do not need altering because they fit me perfectly. The image garments are my favorite color; it's what I like and, most importantly, it represents the One who designed it for me—God—because He created me.

We have to stop letting others design our garments for us; even with their best intentions, their image is still wrong. It may look good to them, but when I look in the mirror, I am not comfortable with what I see because I know on the inside it was not designed for me. Understanding who you are and loving the image God has designed for you takes time. I have learned that it does not happen overnight. In fact, it took me until the age of forty-seven to start understanding I have been wearing the wrong image garments. In this confession, I will tell you that I did not change the garments right away. It took about two years, a lot of crying, lost relationships, lost friendships, and acceptance of my purpose before I even thought about a wardrobe change.

What I realized is that I had become comfortable in the image garments that everyone had chosen for me. Even if they did not fit, I altered them to fit because I liked the garments and people accepted me in them because those individuals were the designers. Those garments came off their personal runways and

I believe those garments can sometimes be a blockage to your being successful in your dreams and goals. When people look at your image, they don't see what God designed; they only see what someone else created for you.

I am not sure when it happened, but I woke up and realized that I am created in God's image and that His image is enough for me to accept the skin I live in. I also learned that when you take off garments that people designed for you, those individuals will feel a certain type of way and will almost make you feel guilty about your change in wardrobe. You have to be adamant about your dreams and goals in order to accept what God has for you. That is what is so great about God; you do not have to worry about it because everything He designs for you is custom made just for you and your journey. All you have to do is accept the skin you're in and understand He made you in His image. I had to learn that people would say a lot of things, but you do not have to accept those words and you do not have to wear them as a garment that defines you. You get to choose what to put on and what to set aside. My confession allows me to accept the skin I am in and to love myself. I had to realize that I am handcrafted and put together by the best. God is the perfect makeup artist, the best hair designer, and the greatest stylist ever to walk the earth and I have full access to Him.

I often tell my students that God blesses us so He can show off His good works through us. He loves to put us on His stage so that people can know that everything I am is because of him. We must allow Him to put us on display. I have to confess that I felt bad that I was not accepting what God wanted for me. I had to repent and tell God I was sorry. Who am I to say what He has for me is not what I want to wear or it's not how I want to represent myself? Very quickly, I learned that I am representing Him, and if it were not for God, I would not be here.

Once the reality set in that I was wasting time growing and developing my gifts, I quickly became a fan of God, my designer! I love me and love my image. Is it perfect? No, but in God's eyes it is, and that is all that matters. I am proud to wear His garments of worship and praise and I wear them well. You don't even have to say anything, people will ask you what you're wearing and who is your designer. It's like being on the red carpet of faith and being interviewed by those who want to know to whom you are connected. They want to know your story, your testimony and once you begin to share it, God will become one of the most sought-after designers because He makes one-of-a-kind image garments and you can only get them by connecting to Him. My image garment is one of faith and determination and it moves your internal motivational meter to push you to your destiny. I want my story to set the stage for all to understand that you do not have to wear other than what God designed for you. Be His prototype, be His muse, let Him dress you. I have learned that I am only what He says I am because I am made in His image. The faith runway is mine to walk!

When you see me walking with confidence and pride, understand I love my image garments as I walk and stride. I have accepted the skin I am in and I love my designer; He creates my garments in my style so that I can wear them for a while. He has graced every magazine and people have talked about Him for years. His greatest runway show was on a cross and everyone was in tears. You can have Him design for you, but you have to accept whatever He creates and just know when you receive your garments, you will walk his faith runway with grace.

See you on the runway!

Tracey L. Sigers

Professor Tracey L. Sigers, MBA, hails from the great state of Ohio where she works for Ohio Christian University as an Affiliate Professor. She holds several degrees, including an MBA and Technology Leadership master's degree from Franklin University. She teaches courses in College Study Skills, Information Technology, Business and in the MBA Program. She also teaches dual credit courses for Reynoldsburg High Schools.

The former Ms. Black Ohio winner is a single mother of two children ages thirty-one and sixteen and two wonderful Blessed Grand's; she has her hands full. She is one of the founders and owners of Iced Treats the Jewelry Company and a member of THE GREATEST SORORITY Alpha Kappa Alpha Incorporated while also using her voice in voice acting, producing voice-overs, commercials, and writing. Tracey also loves football and traveling! This wonder woman has also added Certified Cycling Instructor to her resume!

Professor Sigers is a member of the New Covenant Believers Church where Bishop Howard Tillman is Pastor. She enjoys teaching and allows her classroom environment to be an opportunity not only for learning but also for transformation. Every student is important to her and it is her goal to make sure she is a dream releaser for each student's destiny. She is also the author of her forthcoming debut, *Confessions of a Beauty Queen,* where she confesses her struggles with accepting the skin she is in. Her busy schedule also includes mentoring and life coaching young women.

Born to Speak Productions was birthed out of her own life transformation. Her goal as a speaker is to motivate and use what God gives her to promote transformation in the lives of others. She has an extensive speaking career as well as training and teaching in both state and academia environments. Her high impact style illuminates her audiences, as she speaks to transform and empower lives one vocal cord at a time!

LATRICE D. SNODGRASS

When the Silence is Too Loud

LATRICE D. SNODGRASS

When the Silence is Too Loud

"Trice, your dad, is dead." After I answered the phone to receive my mother's call, those were the words I heard. My heart dropped, and my mind went blank. I was in a space somewhere between reality and insanity. I jumped in my car and headed to the hospital. As I was in route, I received another call that he was not dead, but it did not look good. I rushed to the hospital in a complete fog, unsure of the stoplights, the turns, the traffic, or the scenery. I walked into the emergency department of the hospital and there my daddy lay, hooked up to equipment and unresponsive. At a loss for words, I could only muster the strength to ask, "What happened?"

My daddy was a constant in my life, my number one supporter, no one was ever prouder of me. His love was unconditional and forever present. He was my cheerleader, my motivator, my voice of reason, and the voice that told me the truth whether I wanted to hear it or not. He always had a "talk" with a moral or a lesson: "Never quit" and "Protect your credit because it is a bad boy" and "Always say please and thank you" and "End every conversation with loved ones with the words 'I love you'" and "Greet and depart with a huge loving hug."

He was not perfect, but he was my daddy and I loved him beyond measure. I could not fathom the thought of him no longer being here. He loved life and life loved him. He touched every generation; he met no strangers and developed lasting friendships. My personality was definitely a clone from my daddy.

I looked at the doctor, and asked, "What is the prognosis?"

He told me that he did not have optimal brain activity and things did not look good.

I could not believe what was happening. I wanted and needed more time. I began to pray.

"Lord, You have the final say and You are still in the miracle-working business; all things are possible, and You can do exceedingly and abundantly more than the rest. You said if I have faith the size of a mustard seed…"

Fast forward two days and my daddy is still hooked up, and multiple brain function tests have been conducted, and he is brain dead (to be precise). My brother made the decision to remove my daddy from life support. This was in alignment with his will, as he and my brother had spoken extensively on his after-death wishes. January 16, 2014 was, by far, one of the worst days of my life.

Days following, I kept repeating in my mind that forty-one years, two months and seven days were not enough. I went through life in a state of devastation and disbelief. At this point, life, as I knew it, had stopped. I was in this horrible abyss of unexplainable grief, but God was keeping me. Day by day, He was keeping me sane. I was navigating life the best I could. Life was painful because I missed him and the reality that he was gone was too much to bear. However, I was able to cling to our last conversation.

He had called me the Friday before his death. Our mode of communication was mainly text, but this day he called. We had a conversation about his new cell phone and that he needed to load his contacts into this new phone. Before getting off the phone, he asked if I had to work the next day.

"Daddy, tomorrow is Saturday," I said, "and you know I don't work on Saturdays."

He paused, and, in an awkward state, he said, "Yeah, yeah, I know."

We exchanged our sentiments of love and hung up. I paused after the call because I was puzzled by his moment of confusion, but I carried on. I now know that God orchestrated that moment in time so that I could hear my daddy one last time. By the way, he passed from a brain hemorrhage, so this might explain his momentary confusion. I was completely devastated, and the devil was attacking my mind through the spirit of fear, anxiety, and depression. I went to work every day and played my role, smiling and pretending to be "okay," although I was having grave difficulty living in my skin and being alone was unbearable. I suffered in silence and clung to mechanisms to cope. One of which was gospel music. One particular song got me through my darkest moments. I played it whenever the silence became deafening and my skin began to crawl with grief. I was able to lose myself in the lyrics of God Held Me Together by Zacardi Cortez. It enabled me to make it through that moment in time and reach the next. Find your "thing" that gives you peace and cling to it; that is my constant reminder.

On top of the struggle of making it through day-to-day life, I was in the process of completing the last leg of my doctoral degree, which was my dissertation. I had to finish this process because my dad was so proud that I was on that journey. I began working on this degree in 2008, but life and work kept getting in the way, so I had not made the necessary progress toward the completion, but one day, following his death, I was reading old text messages and noticed that text after text he referred to me as Doc Grass. This was a play on our family surname of Snodgrass, and at that moment, I made a promise that I would dedicate myself to the process and complete the journey for my pops. He knew I could, so I would.

Fast forward one year and about six days, the matriarch of our family went home to be with the Lord at the glorious age of 101. This was my mother's mother, whose family and friends lovingly referred to as Sugamoma. This was an emotional blow, but she had lived a good life, and though my heart ached, I was at peace, as I knew I could not have her forever. Nevertheless, it reopened the wounds of the loss of my daddy, but I kept pressing through life, wearing my mask. I was still pretending to be okay even though every day and every minute the fear of death consumed my life, which pushed me into severe anxiety attacks and bouts with depression that I referred to as grief attacks. I was an emotional basket case, but only in private. I could not allow others to know that I was suffering and coming undone. I did not want anyone to think I was incapable of performing my job. My career was on an upswing, and I could not afford to have anyone doubting my abilities. There is a horrible stigma attached to mental illness that is not attached to any other illness and, as a God-fearing Black woman, I learned not to "claim" things of this nature, to take "it" to the Lord in prayer. I had to be strong because too many people depended upon me to keep it together. So, I suffered in silence and just "dealt with it."

Three weeks following the death of my maternal grandmother, I lost my mother's brother. Uncle Joe and I loved to roller skate, and he and I bonded over this common hobby. We travelled to various cities and states to skate. Over the previous five years, he and I had become extremely close. The weekend before his death, we were on a skate trip. Once again, God intervened to ensure I had additional quality time. This was far too much for my heart and, more significantly, my mind to bear. I experienced three significant deaths in a twelve-month time frame! I could no longer suffer alone because the Silence Was Too Loud. I felt like I was losing my mind. Death consumed my thoughts. I remembered that when my mother was in her early forties, she had a horrible bout with depression. She had a mini breakdown, and I knew I had to get help.

I could no longer suffer in silence because I could not afford to have a nervous breakdown. Through my employer, we had access to an Employee Assistance Program, and I took advantage of the benefit. I selected a faith-based therapist to usher me through this process and help provide clarity. I continued to pray and rely on God, but I knew I needed more. I then began to speak openly with others about my struggle because I did not want anyone else to have to suffer in silence.

Over the years since my father's death, I have heard of brown people, young and old, taking their lives because they suffered in silence. We must remove the stigma from mental illness, and we must encourage our family and friends to pray and seek help. God has blessed professionals with the abilities and skill set to help us get through the most challenging times in life. I still struggle with fear, anxiety and depression, but I never want to be in a place where the silence is too loud, so I openly talk about it in hopes that I will help myself while helping others. The Lord has shown me favor and mercy, as one of my fears was stagnating my career if I sought help, but that was not the case.

In December 2015, I conferred my Doctoral Degree. In October 2017, I obtained a Senior Leadership position in my field and I am in the process of starting my blog to bring awareness and begin to eradicate the stigma surrounding Mental Health Disorders. Mental illness does not discriminate so if it touches your life, please do not suffer alone because you do not have to bear that burden in the loudness of the silence.

I would like to leave you with the following words of encouragement. "When you pass through the waters, I will be with you; and when you pass through the rivers, they will not sweep over you. When you walk through the fire, you will not be burned; the flames will not set you ablaze," Isaiah 43:2.

Dr. LaTrice Snodgrass serves as Chief Operations Officer at AxessPointe, a Federally Qualified Health Center with five locations in Northeast Ohio, and she serves as an Adjunct Professor at Indiana Wesleyan University. She has more than twenty years of leadership experience in healthcare roles. Her published works include a focus on employee engagement, servant leadership, and emotional intelligence topics. She received her Doctorate of Healthcare Administration from the University of Phoenix in 2015 and a Master of Science in Management with a concentration in Healthcare Management in 2005 from Troy State University as well as her Bachelors of Science in Criminal Justice in 2004. She serves on the Board of Trustees at Choices a Community Social Center and is the President of the ADM Support Levy Board. She volunteers at the Akron-Canton Food Regional Food Bank, the Haven of Rest and Habitat for Humanity.

LAVONIA M. THOMPSON

No Matter What, He Still Loves You

LAVONIA M. THOMPSON

No Matter What, He Still Loves You

"God is Love," —John 4:16 (KJV)

First, it was...

"Ma, wake up! It's five o'clock in the evening, what are you doing asleep?"

"I don't know, I'm just so sleepy and tired."

Then, it was...

"Ma, you just ate! Why are you eating again?"

"I don't know, I'm just so hungry."

My mother is not the one to take naps, and she eats like a bird, only a very small serving at a time. So, I knew something wasn't right. She was taking naps and eating like she was crazy. I just didn't know what it was, until it hit me. She had a record of getting pregnant with tied, burned, and clipped tubes. Yet, I didn't think that would happen in her fifties. That was it!

And...

"Ma, you are pregnant!"

She said so confidently, loud and clear, "The devil is a liar! It may stand in line, but it won't march!" We fell out laughing.

Still, she continued taking naps and eating like food was going to leave the earth.

I even told Papa, "You know Mama is pregnant, you just said you wanted another baby around, now you've got it."

Smiling as usual, he said with his Indian accent, "Well, dear, we just gotta do what we gotta do."

Standing there with a strange look on her face, Mama replied, "You might as well get that smile off your face, because we are not having another baby."

The entire family joined in on picking on my mom. I had my daughter and siblings picking on her every chance we got.

A few Sundays later, we were doing our usual, watching movies. I started realizing I had a keen sense of smell. I could smell food a mile away. Candles seemed as if they were lit up in my head. Laundry detergent in my clothes was like it was just poured all over me. I wondered what was going on.

Then, I heard a still voice say, "You are the one pregnant."

I ignored it, like, yeah right.

Then, another voice said, "Did your cycle come this month?"

I ignored that voice, too.

Another voice whispered, "Remember when you called out of work last month because you were sick, throwing up that morning?"

This time, both my ears stood at attention, like two soldiers in the Army. It hit me big, like a TKO in the first round: "Oh my, God, I'm the one pregnant!" I was in denial. I did not tell anyone. I kept picking on my mom, as if she were the one. She kept taking naps and eating as if she were starving.

A week later, I stopped by the store to pick up a pregnancy test. When I got home and took the test, it came out very positive, very quick. I thought to myself, *Well, I know I'm not pregnant, this lil' cheap test playing games on me.*

The next day, I went to CVS and picked up two expensive tests. I took both of them and what did I get? Positive and positive. It was now evident that I was pregnant and my mom was sharing my symptoms with me. I was dreading it, but I had to tell my mom.

I called her up and said, "Ma, I need to talk to you."

"What, I'm cooking?" Go figure, she was hungry and now I knew why.

"I need you to come to my house," I said. "I really need to tell you something." I'm sure I probably scared her to death.

She came right over. We sat down in my living room.

"Ma, I'm pregnant."

I really think a hyena was somewhere in my house. She laughed and laughed uncontrollably.

"Ma, I'm for real."

Still laughing, she said, "I know you are!" She then regained her composure and said, "See, that's why you don't mess and pick with God's children." Then, it started again, laughing hysterically.

Then, the pregnancy blues kicked in and I burst out crying and sobbing like my world had literally come to an end. That was the only thing stopped her from laughing. As a matter of a fact, she started crying. Straight from laughing to crying, just like that. So now, both of us were sobbing and crying our hearts out.

Once we finally got ourselves together, I said, "I can't have this baby."

"Why not?"

"You know the father and I are not on good terms right now."

I'd found out he had been cheating on me, but was always accusing me. We argued more than talking with sense. We didn't spend much time together anymore. The list goes on and on. Our relationship had truly gone downhill, quick.

"Well," she started, "this may be the one thing that will get you two on good terms and on the right path. A baby is a blessing from God. After all, you are thirty-five and you wanted another baby. You know you are not a spring chicken."

"Not like this though, Ma."

"Like what?"

"Another baby out of wedlock."

Of course, at that point, she could get the encouragement speech award of the year because she knew everything to say to help me feel better about everything.

"Have you told him?" she asked me.

We both started crying, *again*.

Through her tears, she asked, "What's wrong now?"

I finally mustered out, "I don't know."

Although, I knew I had let my Father God, Lord Jesus Christ and Holy Spirit down again. I began looking back instead of forward. My first real relationship as an adult was the unwed union that gave me my first born, a beautiful, now twelve-year-old daughter. I thank my Father God for her daily. This same relationship also led me to another relationship I never thought I would experience, meeting and getting to know my Lord and Savior Jesus Christ. This relationship was the best thing that ever happened to me. I walked and talked with Him every day, all day. I kept my Bible on me at all times. I finally realized the meaning of why God's Word is referred to as the daily bread. Some days I went without eating, only reading my Bible for breakfast, lunch, and dinner. My relationship with my Savior and His word was filling me up with the strength, faith, hope and love I needed to keep my sanity, break free and overcome.

My relationship with my daughter's father ended and I made a vow to the Lord that I would remain abstinent until marriage.

I had been a counselor for several years, counseling teens on teen pregnancy prevention and constantly stating, "Abstinence is the only one hundred percent birth control and the only sure way not to contract an STD, STI, or HIV/AIDS and wait for marriage." So, I embarked on that journey and I can honestly say I went several years strong remaining abstinent. I turned down getting to know some great guys. I was not ready for another relationship nor premarital sex, again. While thinking back on all of this, I had to coax my mind back to the present. The first thing I had to do was repent. I cried tons of tears and sent up millions of prayers and begged for forgiveness.

Then, I had to tell my boyfriend I was pregnant. It went okay at first, before he let me know in many actions he did not want to be with me anymore and I was not going to have his support with this baby. He even had the nerve to tell someone it wasn't his baby, which led to my thinking about something I had never done before, something I thought I would never have to do, especially at age thirty-five. I made a life or death decision. I asked my mother and grandmother to accompany me to a clinic.

We left early one Thursday morning. I sat in the back seat with so many different thoughts going through my head. I talked to the Lord all the way. I even said, "Father God, if for any reason You do not want me to go through with this abortion today, please give me a sign or put a stop to it some kind of way. I know You have the power to do that in the name of Jesus." Nothing happened on the way. We made it there safe and sound. No traffic, no sudden stops, no cut offs, no road blocks, no nothing, just a smooth ride to our destination.

When I entered inside, this place was so bland and crowded. No pictures or vibrant colors on the wall. Just plain and simple. The only thing on the wall was a flat screen t.v. There were so many women in there for different reasons, but for the same reason. Like me, they were there to have an abortion. After I was checked in, I had to go to the back into another room filled with women. It was as if I walked into a room of staleness with women that were stiff with no emotions nor strength to even open their mouths to say *hello.* I quickly forgot about why I was there and began to feel so heartbroken to see so many women looking down and depressed. No one was smiling nor making any kind of conversation or anything. You would think they had already had gone through the procedure. My being the person that I am, I started talking to one of the young ladies there. Next thing I knew, the room brightened up. We were telling our reasons for being there. One woman was pregnant by a married man, one was in college and she and her boyfriend wanted to finish school more than have a baby, one already had five children, and could not afford another child. As we continued to talk, we heard a young lady scream aloud. I started thinking, *Now Lord is this one of your signs?* It made some of us instantly say, "I can't do this." But, we all hung in there together.

So finally, it was my turn and I did it. I had an abortion. It was such an unfamiliar, very painful process. I screamed loudly in excruciating pain while the nurse was holding my hand telling me to be calm and everything was going to be alright. All I could do afterward was just sit there and cry and cry. Every tear that rolled down my cheeks, I could feel it roll down my heart, too. Little did I know, this was going to be a huge turning point in my life.

I often hear people say, "Don't look back." I have a saying: "It's okay to look back, just look back to what pushed you forward." I had to look back to what pushed me forward, the relationship with my Father God, Lord Jesus Christ and Holy Spirit. Through the trinity relationship, I learned a lot, and I began to remember who made me fearfully and wonderfully. Not only that, He made me on purpose with a purpose and I could not let this abortion, anyone, or anything else I had been through get in the way of that any longer. I had to dig deep within my soul and get over what I had done really quickly, before I would allow it to take me down further than I already was. Like Tyler Perry's character Brown says, "I said, 'Self,' self said 'huh?' And, I said to myself, 'No matter what anyone thinks or says, no matter when, where or how, no matter what, He still loves you. God is love. God is good! God is not like man! All things work together for my good. I have been called. I have been chosen. I have a purpose. I have the victory through my Lord and Savior Jesus Christ.'"

Now, since I had the abortion, I had to abort a lot of other things in my life to keep moving me forward into my purpose.

LaVonia M. Thompson is a Christian single mother of one daughter, whom she loves dearly. She enjoys spending her free time writing and with her family. Before starting her own consulting business and co-owning a restaurant, she was a youth counselor for over ten years. She has endured a long list of life experiences and lessons that continues to push her into her earthly purpose. She is well on her way of becoming a Certified Christian Life Coach with a Niche of Exhortation, an advocate for women's rights and much more. This project was the start of a new beginning in her life with a purpose of helping other women to break free from bondage, overcome and prevent initial and second abortions. You can enjoy more of this story and a positive, life transformation in her upcoming novel, "A Single Woman's Right to Abort". Through all of her life experiences, she has learned some of the most valuable lessons in life, such as to forgive, laugh, love, live then do it all over again, forgive, laugh, love live.

CAROLYN TREADWELL

Get Out! Live Your Life Intentionally

CAROLYN TREADWELL

Get Out! Live Your Life Intentionally

"I am come that they might have life, and that they might have it more abundantly,"— John 10:10 (KJV)

Are you living your life abundantly? Do you find yourself just settling for where you are, even though you feel you are capable of doing so much more? Or, maybe you have allowed past hurts, disappointments, and failed attempts to paralyze your thoughts. Are you where you are because you have allowed others to define your destiny? Living abundantly scripturally means living a life more fully. In Christ, we live abundantly by His grace with the ability to love, to be at peace, to enrich the lives of others, to overcome evil, and to be free. The power is within us and we have to be consciously aware of every moment. Every aspect of our lives must be approached with a purpose and intentions.

In the 2017 movie *Get Out*, writer and director Jordan Peele introduces the audience to the protagonist Chris Washington who, on the surface, has a normal life. He is a photographer with "the eye" or talent for capturing exquisite details in his photographs. He has a girlfriend with whom he trusts, and no doubt have shared intricate and painful memories of his past. On the surface, there is no indication that he has any problems that could be a potential use to enslave him. Yet, there is a breach as he is placed under hypnosis and his consciousness is banished to the "sunken place," a placed described as a realm deep in the mind where a person's body is paralyzed and crushed by the weight of past mental anguish. If he does not "get out," he will be there permanently. Ironically, it's others that see value in his natural abilities and they want to take it. There is a point in the movie where someone asks Chris, "What is your purpose?" He doesn't have an answer, as he stumbles over his words. In the midst of his vulnerability at that moment, he is summoned to the sunken place with just one simple action.

"For I know the thoughts that I think toward you, saith the Lord, thoughts of peace, and not of evil, to give you an expected end," —Jeremiah 29:11 (KJV)

God has a plan for our lives; we do have a purpose. Are you doing all God has purposed for you to do? Are your thoughts in alignment with His purpose and will for your life? These are important questions for us to answer. We live in a world today full of distractions that shift our focal point to all that we are not or can be. Thus, the expectations we have for ourselves are constantly shifting. We begin to look at life through stained or tainted eyes. In other words, we limit ourselves to a fragmented life because we don't connect with who we are from our soul; we attempt to piece it together from how we view others. We fill our minds with imagery of how others are living, or what others are doing so much that we are blind to how that impacts our ability to be all that we can be. How often do we evaluate ourselves on the basis of our feelings rather than what God says? God is the source of our identity and we were created to live a peaceful and prosperous life.

We all have a divine purpose. Each person has talent and skills uniquely that contribute to the fulfillment of their life's mission. When we are not living within our purpose holistically, we are incomplete as an individual. We are not operating from a point of wholeness. From one moment to the next, we never know what circumstances we will face. There are many subtle things that happen in our lives that can rob us of the opportunity to be all that we can be. What are some things that divert us from our true identity? As children, our parents raised us with their ideals, beliefs, and values. Then, people we meet at work, schools, and religious organizations shape our thoughts. This is not to suggest their guidance, as we begin this journey of life, is meant to harm us. We are not born with an instruction manual, so we need these relationships to build a foundation for living. However, we need to create our own pathway. Our determination to be successful should come from an internal thought process that guides us. Why? If our thoughts are not truly ours—meaning we have not affirmatively identified and developed our own set of beliefs and values—we are not being authentic. In fact, we are living subconsciously as someone else. Stay there too long and we will go through life just living by the script that others have written for us. It is not necessarily a bad script—it is just not ours.

Unfortunately, we can drift into this space where nothing has meaning to us and we care less and less about self. What we do no longer matters, but it does have an impact on our outcomes. We can become bitter, angry, jealous, unforgiving, and hateful. If we don't find a way to *get out,* we will be there lost in a darkened space of self-inflicted adversity. The transformation happens so subtly that we don't notice it. If we are not paying attention, we will find ourselves in that sunken place, settling for a lower standard of living. It is important to understand that if we are not living to our full potential, we are leaving ourselves open to vulnerability that can be easily manipulated by those who can do us harm. Whether we call it a "sunken place," depression, or "darkness," we have reached a point in our lives where we are paralyzed in fear or pain.

I vividly recall the morning I woke up, and realized I did not know the person looking back at me in the mirror. It was the scariest time in my life. A series of life events left me in a world where I was no longer a wife, a daughter, or a mother as it had been scripted for me. Now, the invisible boundaries were quite apparent. In my moment of darkness, my perception of the world no longer existed, I was adrift, hearing only the voices of the past. There were things that had happened in my life that were so painful, it's no wonder I had trouble defining purpose. In my lifetime, I have had many traumatic events that has filled my mind with thoughts of guilt, hopelessness, weakness, and failures. I buried the pain of sexual abuse, miscarriages, stillbirth, divorces, career disasters, and the death of my parents. My coping mechanism was filling my life with doing stuff. I crammed every minute of my days with some form of activity; pushing back the pain and always presenting myself strong and confident. I worked full-time, went to school full-time, and volunteered for several activities at school and church.

Some years back, my mother posed a question to me before she passed away: "Are you living or just existing?" I knew the answer to the question the moment I learned she died. I answered it—I was just existing. For several years after that moment I was entrapped in a place of darkness and despair. I was in the "sunken place." All my emotions—sorrow, pain, anger and fear—collided, leaving me unable to move forward. For the first time in my life, I was experiencing loneliness, depression, hatred, and guilt. I was literally sitting in the middle of my bed, dealing with all the events from my past. I felt trapped because I knew mentally, spiritually, and physically I could no longer keep up the charade of enjoying life. It was time to acknowledge the bad things that had happened to me and begin the process of healing.

I was molested at the age of nine years old by my stepfather. I learned how to avoid the pain by developing routines and habits that kept me in motion. Because I did not want people to make fun of me, be angry, or blame me for what happened, I stayed silent. This one transgression against me shaped my perception of life and the many decisions that had me doubting, hating, and rejecting myself. How do I get out of this "sunken place?" Remember, the sunken place is deep in the mind. There is a saying that is true both from a scientific and spiritual perspective: Light trumps darkness. The answer I was seeking was right before me all the time. The Bible says, in John 11: 10 KJV, *"If a man walk in the night, he stumbleth, because there is no light in him."* For many years, I followed my carnal reasoning for not bringing to light what was happening to me in the dark. Of course, as a child, fear of rejection by mother had overcome me. The mother-daughter relationship is the most powerful bond in the world because it sets the stage for all other relationships. Those encounters with my stepfather led me to believe my mother did not love me. In my adolescent years, the incidents still haunted me and then I began blaming myself because I should have stood up to him. Even as an adult, it has been hard to bring this transgression against me to light because, again, I allowed myself to believe the failed marriages, miscarriages, sickness, financial woes, and the death of my mother were all punishment for me not rejecting my stepfather. I was relying on my own reasoning and strategy for getting past the pain of my past. It was what I call "surface living," just existing.

1 John 1:5 (KJV) says, *"God is light and in him no darkness all. It turns out that I have the power to turn on the light through prayer, repentance and forgiveness."* Jesus said, *"I am the light of the world: he that followeth me shall not walk in darkness, but shall have the light of life,"* 1 John 8:12 (KJV). The devil wants to keep us trapped in this veil of darkness. The scriptures say, "*he is seeking to devour us*" (1 Peter 5:8). He will use any means necessary to keep you from enjoying what God has planned for you. Jesus said he came that we may have life more abundantly. In other words, He comes that we may have life in Him that is meaningful, purposeful, joyful, and eternal. We receive this abundant life the moment we accept Jesus as our Savior. This is what I call "Intentional Living." Living life intentionally begins with knowing God and his purpose for our lives. Intentional living is a continual process of learning and maturing spiritually. God will pour into us the light source that we need to illuminate in those times of darkness where failure, pain, and sorrow linger. Intentional living revolves around our taking the steps to grow in the grace and knowledge of the Lord and Savior Jesus Christ. Ultimately, an abundant life will prevent us from struggling with sin and doubt. When we live congruently with how God created us to love and forgive ourselves as well others, we cast out the darkness with our light. Get Out! Live your life intentionally for God.

Carolyn Treadwell is an independent certified leadership coach, speaker, and trainer for the John Maxwell Group. She is also an author and organization development consultant with twenty-five years of experience in corporate training, performance management, leadership, and organizational development. In her role as a consultant, she assists business leaders in structuring organizational vision and mission that are in alignment with the desired business outcomes. She has earned a doctorate in Organizational Leadership from Northcentral University and a Master Degree in Public Administration with a specialization in Program Development & Analysis from the University of Illinois.

Visit her website at http://www.johncmaxwellgroup.com/carolynbutler/

MISSY WATTS-RODRIGUEZ

Broken No More

MISSY WATTS-RODRIGUEZ

Broken No More

"In the day when I cried Thou answeredst me, and strengthenedst me with strength in my soul."
— Psalm 138:3 KJV

People come to know God in different ways. At the tender age of nine years old, I had encounters with Him in my bedroom closet. Yes in my bedroom closet. This is where I would hide and He would meet me there. I didn't really know God before that and I certainly didn't know Jesus at all. But, somehow, I knew God was real and that He knew me, the scared, broken little girl. I was so shattered inside from abuse. I can remember crying and asking God to please take me to heaven with Him so that I would be safe from any more harm. How did I know that I would be safe with Him when I barely knew much about Him at all? Because He knew me.

"For Thou hast possessed my reins: Thou hast covered me in my mother's womb. I will praise Thee; for I am fearfully and wonderfully made: marvelous are Thy works; and that my soul

knoweth right well. My substance was not hid from Thee, when I was made in secret, and curiously wrought in the lowest parts of the earth. Thine eyes did see my substance, yet being unperfect; and in Thy book all my members were written, which in continuance were fashioned, when as yet there was none of them."
—Psalm 139: 13-16

Not long after, God sent a wonderful woman into my young life that offered to take me to church on Sundays. She taught Sunday school and children's group as well. Quite the "Mama Goose" she was! Looking back, I realize that she was sent to plant the seed of God's Word in my heart.

Now let's fast forward to my teenage years. This is where the real fun began! I grew up in a small, rural town on the northern tip of the Outer Banks of North Carolina. Knotts Island is a coastal town and very country at the same time. Wetlands and cornfields. Not too much going on there. AT ALL. Not much to get into except for trouble. I jumped head first into it by the time I was sixteen years old. We all know the term sweet sixteen. In my case, it was more like senseless sixteen. I discovered boys, alcohol, and drugs. I couldn't get enough. The irresistible lure of the quick fix took hold. In our brokenness, we crave these quick fixes because we believe the lie that they will remedy the pain we carry inside. I didn't realize what was going on at the time. At the age of nineteen, I became pregnant by my boyfriend. He wanted to marry me and raise our child together. I was young and very scared. The thought of becoming a mother at that age was something I couldn't bear to wrap my brain around. It was inconceivable to me. I went through with the abortion procedure. As we walked into the clinic, protestors yelled out to me to please reconsider my decision and that they would be willing to take my baby. Back then, I thought they were crazy and out of line for such behavior. Now I believe it's quite possible they understood the true value and purpose of a human life. Many years after my abortion, I would come to realize just how very damaged I was inside due to the choice I made. My brokenness became much worse than it already was. It is now my belief that abortion equals one dead and one severely wounded. Emotionally, mentally, and often times, physically. When I was in labor with my son many years later, my cervix would not dilate more than five centimeters due to scar tissue that remained from the abortion procedure. Fortunately, my son was born without complication via C-Section.

"Reproach hath broken my heart; and I am full of heaviness: and I looked for some to take pity, but there was none; and for comforters, but found none."
—Psalm 69:20

I have learned that we look for things to serve as Band-Aids to cover up our pain. But that's just it. It's all just a cover up. This became a vicious cycle for me well into my twenties and thirties. I was notorious for starting things and not finishing them. I changed careers more times than we change our outfits getting ready for a date night ladies! I was never content in my quest for inner peace. What a hot mess I was! Two failed marriages, alcohol/drug abuse, two failed suicide attempts, and always searching for the next "Band-Aid" to make me feel better about myself. My life was a train wreck for the most part. All I could figure is that there had to be some type of protective force field wrapped around me and it wouldn't be long before I would find out who He was.

"But God commandeth His love toward us, in that, while we were yet sinners, Christ died for us."
—Romans 5:8

Over the years, I had the pleasure of experiencing some fantastic adventures. There were a lot of good days, believe it or not. Many of them were spent serving as a flight attendant for two airlines. Nothing like seeing Paris, France in the springtime! But I have to tell you that there is one adventure in life I have loved the very best. It's this journey Jesus Christ has had me on. I met Him in November of 2000 and I've not been the same since. He met me right where I was. Hot mess and all! I thought I knew what love was until I met Him. I would soon find out that my concept of love was very distorted and not really love at all.

"For God so loved the world, that He gave His only begotten Son, that whosoever believeth in Him should not perish, but have everlasting life."
—John 3:16

"But God, Who is rich in mercy, for His great love wherewith He loved us, even when we were dead in sins, hath quickened us together with Christ (by grace ye are saved)."
—Ephesians 2: 4-5

"In this was manifested the love of God toward us, because that God sent his only begotten Son into the world, that we might live through Him. Herein is love, not that we loved God, but that He loved us, and sent His Son to be the propitiation for our sins. Beloved, if God so loved us, we ought also to love one another."
—1 John 4: 9-11

God's love is not like ours. His love is pure and unconditional. This amazing love would change me forever. Jesus Christ took hold of my life. He loved me too much to leave me the way that I was. The deep-rooted brokenness inside of me that I operated from was no match for Jesus. His love, grace, and mercy saw the best in me and only He could bring it forth. This is true love!

"Charity suffereth long and is kind; charity envieth not; charity vaunteth not itself, is not puffed up, doth not behave itself unseemly, seeketh not her own, is not easily provoked, thinketh no evil; rejoiceth not in iniquity, but rejoiceth in the truth; beareth all things, endureth all things."
—1 Corinthians 13:4-7

It still amazes me that through it all, God knew the plan He had for my life. He didn't change His mind about me. Over the years, Jesus has peeled back the layers of my soul to reveal the roots of brokenness within me that could no longer remain. For many of those years, I was very full of unforgiveness and bitterness. By peeling back the layers of my soul, Jesus showed me that I was operating from this ugly root in the way that I handled the relationships in my life. It is a certain kind of inner torture we inflict upon ourselves. The truth of the matter is that it's more like being trapped inside a cold prison cell in your own heart. I couldn't carry it all anymore. Forgiveness is key in the process of healing brokenness. We can forgive others with the help of the One that truly understands what it's like to suffer and still forgive. Jesus gets us! If we allow Him to, He will continue to change us from glory to glory.

"And we know that all things work together for good to them that love God, to them who are called according to His purpose."
—Romans 8:28

ALL things. I believe that all things mean the good and the bad things in life. Yes, the bad things, too. The trauma we've endured, our failures, our bad choices, etc. In the healing of our brokenness, Jesus teaches us to use what we've learned to help and encourage others. In this, we step into our purpose and our destiny.

"Wherefore comfort yourselves together, and edify one another, even as also ye do."
—1 Thessalonians 5:11

Be encouraged, dear heart. God is intentional. He is not finished with you and me yet!

Missy Watts-Rodriguez is a Professional Life Coach, Christian Life Coach, and Medical Training Instructor. She has one son and makes her home on the Outer Banks of North Carolina. Her favorite activities include reading, learning new things, fishing, playing in the ocean, and spending quality time with friends and family. She is passionate about inner healing and wholeness for women of all ages.

Write Your Own Story

____

(Your Name)

____

(Story Title)

(Your Name)

(Story Title)

Your Name: ______________________________

Story Title: ____

Your Name: ________________________________

Story Title: ____

Your Name: ______________________________

Made in the USA
Lexington, KY
01 March 2018